Do Voters
Look to the Future?

Do Voters Look to the Future?

Economics and Elections

Brad Lockerbie

State University of New York Press

170203723

Published by State University of New York Press, Albany

© 2008 State University of New York

For information, address State University of New York Press, Albany, NY
www.sunypress.edu

Production by Ryan Morris
Marketing by Michael Campochiaro

Library of Congress Cataloging-in-Publication Data

Lockerbie, Brad, 1961–
    Do voters look to the future? : economics and elections / Brad Lockerbie.
       p. cm.
    Includes bibliographical references and index.
    ISBN 978-0-7914-7481-5 (hardcover : alk. paper)   1. Voting—United States.
2. Elections—United States.   3. Presidents—United States—Election.   4. United States—Congress—Elections.   5. United States—Economic conditions.   I. Title.
    JK1967.L63 2008
    324.973—dc22

                                         2007036635

10 9 8 7 6 5 4 3 2 1

To my wife,
Barry Lockerbie,
and to my stepson,
Sam Knell

Contents

Illustrations

Acknowledgments

This book grew out of a long desire to understand why people vote the way they do. At times, this project has seemed like a lifelong endeavor. Nonetheless, I am pleased that I went on the exploration.

The National Election Study and the Survey of Consumer Attitudes and Behavior data for this project were made available by the Inter-University Consortium for Social and Political Research. The data on congressional elections were made available by *Congressional Quarterly Weekly Report*. Neither organization bears any responsibility for my use of the data.

There are, of course, many people to thank for the help with this project. I have benefitted from the counsel of many people. First, my desire to understand the role of expectations in political behavior was stimulated in graduate school by Arthur H. Miller, Michael S. Lewis-Beck, and Richard G. Niemi. The discussions I had with each of them were very fruitful. Second, several colleagues at the University of Georgia helped to make this book a better product. Charles S. Bullock III, Robert Grafstein, and John A. Maltese read drafts of various chapters, made comments, and had discussions with me that helped to clarify the manuscript. Third, Stephen A. Borrelli, a frequent coauthor and a good friend from graduate school, has talked with me about this project more than he probably would care to have done. I am honored to call all of them colleagues. I would also like to thank Michael Rinella and Amanda Lanne from State University of New York Press for putting up with my questions and requests for assistance. Dana Foote copyedited the final draft of this manuscript. She made me look like a much better writer than I am. Also, Ryan Morris, the production editor, put up with the many questions I had. Last, I would like to thank the anonymous reviewers who provided me with insights on this project. None of those aforementioned, of course, bear any culpability for anything here. I assume responsibility for the aspects that are flawed.

I would be remiss if I did not thank my wife, Barry Lockerbie, for her assistance with this project. She lit the fire under me to get this project completed. Without her, the project would have taken much longer to complete. For that, among other things, I am grateful. My stepson, Sam Knell, was a joy, most of the time, while I was working on this project. There is nothing like a little boy to keep you from getting too full of yourself.

Chapter 1

Introduction

W hy people vote the way they do is one of the most often asked questions in political science. We ask this important question because it is both interesting and vexing. Voting behavior holds such an important place in political science, for it is seemingly the clearest avenue to test theories of democracy. Are the people of a democracy living up to the ideals of democratic theory?[1] Do citizens make reasoned and informed choices? Are our governors constrained by the actions, or potential actions, of the electorate? If the answer to any of these questions is no, we want to know why. Not only do we want to know why, we want to know what these answers mean for democratic governance. Why do voters act the way they do? In short, is democracy working? In *The American Voter* (Campbell et al. 1960), one of the first major social-psychological examinations of vote choice to examine these questions in a systematic manner, the view of the electorate put forward is not a terribly complimentary one. The authors depict the voter as driven by a long-term, largely unthinking, attitude, namely party identification. This attitude is acquired via childhood socialization, well before the acquisition of other political information. Moreover, according to the authors, party identification is largely immune to change. It is the unmoved mover. Certainly, the authors consider forces other than party identification. The two presidential elections preceding publication of their work had a Republican candidate winning election and reelection, at a time when the Democratic Party had a decided advantage in party identification. If a Republican could win the White House, something in addition to party identification had to be influencing voting behavior. The authors argue that short-term forces could win over the votes of some portion of the electorate. Some partisans could be swayed by short-term forces, and independents, without the anchor of party identification, could more easily be swung over to one side. The swing voters are political independents and those who are not firmly anchored to a party. Lacking short-term forces working against them, a Democrat would win the presidency. With short-term forces on the side of a Democratic candidate for the presidency, the Democratic Party would win in a landslide.

Since the publication of *The American Voter* (Campbell et al. 1960), many authors have taken this view to task. Many researchers have revised upward their view of the American electorate. Scholars have examined the role issues play in voting behavior (Jackson 1975; Markus and Converse 1979; Nie and Anderson 1974; Nie, Verba, and Petrocik 1976; Page and Jones 1979; Repass 1971; et al.). Other researchers have focused on the role of retrospective evaluations as an explanation of vote choice. Most notably, Key (1966) and Fiorina (1981a) argue that voters reward (punish) the incumbent administration for good (bad) performance while in office. If times have been good (bad), the voter rewards (punishes) the incumbent party by voting to retain (reject) it. Chappell and Keech (1985), in a much more sophisticated version of the retrospective model, argue that voters look at the actions of government, anticipate the consequences of present government action, and vote accordingly. If the actions of the incumbent party are likely to lead to economic good (bad) times, the incumbent is rewarded (punished) at the ballot box. Note that in these arguments, the role of the opposition party is relatively modest.[2] The opposition party does not offer any vision for the future. Instead, the smart opposition party merely points out what can be perceived as the failings of the incumbent administration. The incumbent party similarly does not offer a vision for the future; instead, it points proudly to past successes.

Still, other work has attempted to build on this research by examining the effects of both retrospective and prospective evaluations on vote choice (Abramowitz 1985; Kuklinski and West 1981; Lewis-Beck 1988a; Lockerbie 1992; Miller and Wattenberg 1985). These researchers argue that voters look at the expected performance of the parties competing for office, among other factors, and vote for the one they believe is going to do the best job in the future.[3]

The focus of the research presented herein is the prospective model of voting behavior. The argument is that voters are calculating individuals who look at both of the parties, decide which one will do a better job in the future, and cast their ballots accordingly. Both the retrospective and prospective models of voting behavior, as commonly tested, hold that voters are rational utility maximizers.[4] What utility are people trying to maximize? As is commonly done, this work assumes people are trying to maximize their financial well-being.[5] Of course, Downs (1957, 36), from whom I borrow the rational actor model, argues that the basic determinant of voting behavior is the stream of benefits derived from government activity.[6] The stream of benefits is not necessarily limited to economic concerns. Downs, instead, includes all benefits, economic and non-economic, in his calculation of the stream of benefits. Why then the focus on economics? Quite simply, money is needed to undertake many of the activities we deem important. Like election is for politicians, financial well-being is a prerequisite for many of the goals we citizens have. Additionally, the gathering and processing of political information is costly.[7] Individuals, to overcome this cost, or difficulty, are likely to economize wherever possible. One means of reducing the costs of collecting and digesting political information is to employ information gathered for other purposes. People will be best informed on those issues that directly influence their economic well-being. Citizens will in all likelihood gather some information in their day-to-day life that might have some bearing on politics. Changes in income are readily apparent, and promises to change one's income are likely to generate greater scrutiny than are promises that do not directly influence one's livelihood.[8] Also, I would not be surprised to find that these evaluations are highly correlated with a more encompassing evaluation of which party is better.

The Retrospective and Prospective Models of Voting Behavior

Of what consequence is it which model of voting behavior (retrospective or prospective) more accurately describes the process by which voters make their decisions? Before answering this question directly, let us consider the assumptions of both models. Both the retrospective and prospective models, as typically presented, assume voters attempt to maximize their economic well-being. The retrospective model assumes a focus on only the past. Key (1966), in *The Responsible Electorate*, argues that voters look to the past because evaluations of the past are concrete. Because these retrospective evaluations are grounded in experienced reality, Key argues that it will be relatively easy for voters to take them into account when deciding which candidate to support in an election. If all is going well (poorly), the voter casts a ballot to retain (reject) the incumbent party. In short, the retrospective model is a reward/punishment theory of voting behavior; the voter does not take the challenger into account. Key (1966) argues that voters are unlikely to make use of prospections because the future is too hazy; voters do not have the wherewithal to predict the future. While Key implies that we can discern what the government bears responsibility for, he also argues that we cannot compare the two parties. If voters can accurately determine the national government's responsibility for the state of the economy, as Key argues, it does not seem to be much of a leap to argue that voters can make comparisons across parties concerning the future. Arguably, determining whether the government is responsible for the state of the economy and determining for what portions of the economy the government bears responsibility is more intellectually demanding than making a forecast of which party will do a better job.

The retrospective model of voting behavior is a satisficing model.[9] If the incumbent party has met (not met) the minimum standards of the voter, the voter casts a ballot to retain (reject) the incumbent party. If the voter is reasonably pleased with the past performance of the incumbent administration, the retrospective model holds that the voter will not kick the incumbent party out of office. Note that not once is the challenging party explicitly taken into account. It is not said that the voter might actually cast a ballot *for* the challenging party instead of against the governing party. Considerations of the opposition party, in the retrospective model, do not influence the voters' calculations.[10] One might quite reasonably argue that the retrospective model is not a rational choice model of voting behavior.[11] If only one option, the incumbent, is considered, a voter has far from complete information. While I would not argue that a voter needs to have complete information to be a rational voter, by that standard there has not been a rational voter nor will there ever be a rational voter. I would argue that making an evaluation of the choices, however cursory, is necessary for one to be counted a rational voter. One must, after all, process some information and there should be a connection between one's preferences and beliefs on the one hand and voting on the other.

The prospective model of voting behavior assumes that people, within the constraints of available alternatives, try to maximize their income. Instead of deciding whether the incumbent party has met some minimum standard, the prospective voter asks which party will perform better in the future. As Downs (1957, 36) states, "each citizen casts his vote for the party he believes *will* provide him with more benefits than any other" (emphasis added). In short, voters look at the available options and attempt to maximize their income by selecting the party under which they will fare best financially in the future.[12]

While the prospective model of voting behavior places higher demands on the voter, it also gives the voter more credit than the retrospective model. Instead of assuming the electorate to be myopic (backward looking), the prospective model assumes the voter to be hyperopic (forward looking).[13] The prospective model, for example, allows a voter to believe that the incumbent party has performed poorly, but the challenging party will perform more poorly than the incumbent party in the future.[14] Bratton (1994), for example, argues that the Republicans were not terribly hurt by the deficit in the presidential election of 1988. Despite the voters' displeasure over the worsening state of the deficit, she finds that many voters were not likely to think that the Democratic candidate would do a better job than the Republican candidate in alleviating the problem. Consequently, the voters did not punish the Republican party's presidential candidate in the general election for what the voters perceived as their poor performance on the issue of the deficit.

One question that should be addressed, though admittedly not completely answered, at this juncture is through what process do voters form expectations. This question alone could well be a book. Needless to say, what I present here will be an exceptionally short and simplified answer. Chapter 2 presents a brief empirical examination of this question. There are three primary means by which voters might form their expectations. The first is a simple extrapolative model. What has happened in the past will happen in the future. If the incumbent has performed well in the past, the incumbent will perform well in the future. If this model is appropriate, then the distinction between the retrospective and prospective models is largely meaningless. If the extrapolative model holds, retrospections will be perfect predictors of prospections.[15] The second is the adaptive expectations model, as formulated by Cagan (1956). This formulation holds that individuals use information concerning past forecasting errors to revise their expectations concerning the future. As the adaptive expectations model is usually presented, the individual uses a weighted average of the past to form expectations of the future. If, for example, one had underpredicted inflation for the last few months, one would, taking these mispredictions into account, begin to revise one's predictions upward. Translating this to the political world, if one had forecast that the incumbent would perform up to some standard and the administration repeatedly had fallen below that standard, one would revise forecasts of the incumbent's performance downward. This formulation of how individuals form expectations is intuitively pleasing, but it does not allow the voter to take new information into account. The individual making these predictions is entirely backward looking. Only past errors cause a revision of expectations.

The third formulation, the rational expectations model, holds that people take new information into account when making forecasts. The following example from Begg (1982, 25–26) illustrates this important difference between the adaptive and rational expectations model.

Suppose that OPEC is meeting next week but that the outcome of their deliberations is a formality; everyone knows that they will announce a doubling of oil prices. Surely economists will be predicting higher inflation from the moment at which news of the oil price increase first becomes available. Yet the hypothesis of Adaptive Expectations asserts that individuals raise inflation expectations only after higher inflation has gradually fed into the past data from which they extrapolate.

Adaptive expectations are entirely myopic. According to the adaptive expectations conception of expectation formation, individuals do not take new information that is readily available into account. Imagine the incumbent has improved one's financial position during his administration, but during the campaign for reelection, the incumbent credibly, and perhaps unwisely from an electoral perspective, proposes some programs that will dig deeply into one's wallet. If one forms expectations from what one has experienced, one will not take this new information into account when evaluating the likely future performance of the incumbent party. One would merely extrapolate from the past, correcting for any past forecasting errors, to arrive at one's expectations of the future performance of the incumbent administration. A voter would not take the campaign promise of the incumbent into account when making a forecast.[16] Under a theory of rational expectations, one would take this new information into account when calculating the expected utility under the new administration. Similarly, under an adaptive expectations model, the voter would not take the opposition party's promises into account. Assume we have a credible candidate promising to take some action with regard to the economic future. Do we expect voters to ignore this information because they have not experienced the results of this action? Imagine a candidate promises to trim the Medicare program and you depend on that program. Similarly, imagine a candidate promises to close a military base where you are employed or that is the perceived economic lifeblood of your community. Should we expect you, the voter, to ignore these promises? Would we expect one to wait until the person is elected and then act surprised when the promise is acted upon? I think not. In fact, the empirical work strongly suggests that voters have good reason to pay attention to the promises of candidates. Fishel (1985) and Royed and Borrelli (1997) find that candidate/party promises are kept.

One objection that is likely to arise at this point is whether information concerning the future is readily available to the typical voter. If this information is not readily available, if it is too costly to obtain, the typical voter might economize by just using information from the past. Minford and Peel (1983) argue that the marginal cost of obtaining such information is sufficiently low as to allow the typical individual to form an opinion about the future of the economy that is more sophisticated than a simple extrapolative or adaptive expectations model would suggest. All one needs to do, according to Minford and Peel (1983), is avail oneself of the forecasts of organizations that the media reports. The information can be picked up quite easily. One does not have to be an econometrician to be able to have a reasonably well-informed opinion of the economy. Also, keep in mind when voting one does not have to know exactly what each party will do, nor does one have to know what the exact results of the actions of the parties will be. All one has to do is figure out which party, if either, one thinks will be better for one's finances. This is a considerably less arduous task than attempting to ascertain the rates of inflation or unemployment, or the direction of change for either.

While in some instances the conclusions one draws about the future will be the same regardless which model of expectation formation members of the electorate employ, there are instances in which the conclusions drawn will differ. Presumably, it is more in keeping with the rational actor model to employ this new information when deciding how to vote in an upcoming election. The inferences one draws from these sets of assumptions differ substantially. Imagine that one blames the incumbent party for current bad times; the retrospective model (either extrapolative or adaptive expections) predicts a vote against the incumbent. If one believes that the incumbent party will do a better job than the opposition, the retrospective model still predicts a vote against the incumbent.[17] Remember, under the retrospective model, only one's disappointment with the past performance of the incumbent administration influences one's vote choice. In fact, the voter, according to the retrospective model, does not make an evaluation of the future. Under this set of conditions, the prospective model, however, predicts a vote for the incumbent, despite the incumbent's poor past performance. If prospective economic evaluations are important in explaining vote choice, a greater responsibility is placed on the parties. Under the retrospective model, all a challenging party has to do is convince the electorate that the incumbent party has performed poorly. Under a prospective model, the challenging party has to convince the electorate that it will, if elected, do a better job than the incumbent party in the future. Similarly, the incumbent party cannot rest upon its laurels if the economy has prospered. The incumbent party will not be retained if it cannot convince a sufficient number of voters that it will do a better job than the opposition in the future. The challenging party still has the opportunity to convince the electorate that it can do an even better job in the future. Thus, past performance is not enough.

What Have We Learned So Far?

The literature is replete with works concerning the role of economics and elections. Monroe (1979) dates the first empirical article as Barnhart's (1925) attempt to explain the rise of the Populist Party during the 1880s and 1890s in terms of drought that led to economic hardship.[18] There have been numerous studies of economic voting at the individual level, with most of that research focusing on retrospective voting. Fiorina (1978), in his analysis of presidential elections from 1956 through 1972, finds only modest support for the hypothesis that members of the electorate base their vote choices on retrospective evaluations. He finds even less support for his model of House elections during presidential election years and no support whatsoever in midterm elections. In fact, in the midterm races, exactly one-half of his economic variables are in the unexpected direction, and three of these are statistically significant.[19]

There is one major problem with Fiorina's (1978) analysis, a problem he freely admits. The American National Election Study retrospective personal economic items he employs are especially noisy indicators of one's opinion concerning the influence of the government on one's finances. The survey item employed by Fiorina (1978) asks respondents if in the past year their personal financial condition has improved, stayed the same, or worsened. Obviously, this question elicits responses that are not related to one's opinion of the government's impact on one's income. Having a child, getting married, receiving a large inheritance, and the like, influence one's financial status, but it is not likely that one would assign responsibility to the government for these changes. Unless one assigns responsibility to the government for all, or most, changes in one's financial well-being, it is unlikely that this indicator will accurately reflect one's opinion of governmentally induced changes in income. Lane (1962), Brody and Sniderman (1977), Feldman (1982, 1985), Kinder and Mebane (1983), and Peffley (1985) have found that most people do not attribute responsibility for all changes in financial status to the government. Instead of assigning responsibility to the government, people have what is called an "ethic of self-reliance." Changes in financial status are one's own responsibility, not some outside entity. Success or failure is due to something the individual does or does not do. If one gets fired, it is one's own fault. If one gets a big raise, it is through the dint of one's effort and ability, not a growing economy or anything else beyond one's control. Economic success and failure are thought to be the result of one's own efforts, not the result of external actors. Consequently, we should not expect a strong relationship between these simple economic items and vote choice.

Using the same questions as Fiorina (1978), Kinder and Kiewiet (1979) report that the personal retrospective economic items fail to attain significance in models of voting behavior in House elections. Their analysis shows, however, that "sociotropic," or collective evaluations of the national economy, consistently play a significant role in explaining vote choice. Similarly, Kinder and Kiewiet (1981) find that these evaluations are significant in explaining vote choice in the 1972 and 1976 presidential and House elections. Many of these "sociotropic" evaluations, like the retrospective items Fiorina (1978) employs, lack a clear political referent. An item that asks the respondent to evaluate the national economy may elicit responses unrelated to the government's management of the economy. An individual may believe the economy is performing poorly, though the poor performance is not a result of the government's action. Instead, the respondent may believe the incumbent administration is doing as good a job as is possible in dealing with a difficult situation. Perhaps the respondent attributes responsibility for economic hard times to a foreign cartel, big business, or big labor. Nonetheless, these items may be significantly related to vote choice if voters are of the opinion the national economy is largely, though not necessarily completely, the responsibility of the national government.[20] Even if voters view the national economy as only being partly influenced by the national government, they might well use the aggregate changes as indicators of government competence. Voters may be of the opinion that individual changes in financial well-being are the result of both the government's actions and idiosyncratic events. It is more likely that people will assign responsibility to the national government for the state of the economy than they will attribute their own well-being to the government, if both types of evaluations lack a political referent. Consequently, evaluations of the national economy are related to vote choice while individual changes in financial well-being, dominated by idiosyncratic factors, are not related to vote choice.

Other items employed by Kinder and Kiewiet (1979, 1981) have a clear political referent, such as the government's management of the economy. Of the items employed by Kinder and Kiewiet, these have the strongest and most consistent findings supporting the economic voting hypothesis.[21] Kramer (1983) argues that these items are significant because Kinder and Kiewiet do not adequately control for partisanship. If anything, Kinder and Kiewiet overcontrol for partisanship. They include party identification, as well as a feeling thermometer differential for the parties, in their vote choice equations. What more they could have done, I do not know. With these overwhelming controls for party identification, it is somewhat surprising that any of their other variables turn up as statistically significant, especially since party identification is responsive to political forces (Fiorina 1981a; Jackson 1975; Lockerbie 1989, 2002; Markus and Converse 1979).

Although the retrospective model has dominated the research examining the influence of economics on elections, there have been attempts to discern the role of prospective economic evaluations (Abramowitz 1985; Fiorina 1981a; Kuklinski and West 1981; Lewis-Beck 1988a, 1988b).[22] It is important to review these works so that we might have a better idea as to the state of the research on this matter.

Kuklinski and West (1981) argue that previous models of voting behavior have been improperly specified due to the omission of prospective economic evaluations, and for this reason, it is not surprising that little evidence of economic voting has been found at the individual level. The findings of Kuklinski and West offer mixed results. In 1978, prospective voting takes place in Senate but not in House elections. While they are to be commended for including the Senate as well as the House, their study is not without problems. First, they examine only one election year, thereby limiting their ability to generalize. A more important problem is the employment of survey items that do not directly reflect evaluations, either retrospective or prospective, of government performance. Just as others have done, the authors do not employ items that include a sense of attribution. They simply look at perceptions of past change and expectations of future change. People are asked if their personal financial well-being has gotten better, worse, or stayed the same over the course of the past year. Similarly, they are asked if they expect the future to bring better, worse, or the same financial times.

Fiorina (1981a), in his book *Retrospective Voting in American National Elections*, attempts to include both retrospective and prospective items that do assign responsibility to the government for changes in the economy.[23] He makes use of items that ask the respondents to evaluate the government's performance in managing the problems of inflation and unemployment for his retrospective measures. The prospective items ask the respondents to state which party, if either, would be better at managing these problems. While there is an attribution of responsibility to the government for the state of economy in these questions, it would be a cleaner test of the hypothesis if these economic items were directly focused on the individual. In these years, unfortunately, there are not any prospective items that have both a sense of attribution of responsibility to the government and a focus on the individual. Fiorina does find a strong prospective bent in the electorate in presidential (1976) and House (1974 and 1976) elections. Like other studies, this one too suffers from having few election years. Our level of confidence in the generalizability of the findings is less than if more years were analyzed. Abramowitz (1985) analyzes the role of retrospective and prospective economic evaluations on voting in House midterm elections of 1974, 1978, and 1982. While he has no positive findings on this front, he does find that these economic evaluations influence presidential approval, which, in turn, influences vote choice strongly. Like many other studies, this one provides limited ability to make generalizations, and the economic items the author employs do not include a sense of attribution.

Lewis-Beck (1988a, 1988b), like some others, argues that previous economic models of voting behavior have been misspecified due to the omission of prospective economic items, and those models, such as Fiorina's (1981a), that claim to employ future oriented items asking which party would better manage the economy are not explicitly future oriented. Lewis-Beck (1988a) argues that the items Fiorina employs are in the conditional, not future, tense.[24] For example, one of Fiorina's items

(1976, 139) is worded as follows: "Do you think the problem of inflation *would* (emphasis added) be handled better by the Democrats, by the Republicans, or about the same by both?" In his analysis of the 1984 elections, Lewis-Beck uses items that clearly direct the respondent toward the future, that is, "Now looking ahead—do you think that a year from now you (and your family there) will be better off financially, or worse off, or just about the same as now?" Lewis-Beck uses a similar item concerning five years in the future. Lewis-Beck's (1988a) findings support the hypothesis that voters cast their ballots with an eye to the future in both presidential and House elections.

While supportive of the contention that voters look to the future when voting and that the voter is capable of differentiating between distinct time frames, there are some difficulties with the strategy Lewis-Beck (1988a) employs. The prospective items Lewis-Beck uses, like many in the subfield, are without a clear political referent. One can imagine a respondent might expect a change in financial status without attributing responsibility to the government. If the government is not the agent expected to cause these changes, there is no theoretical reason to expect these prospective evaluations to influence vote choice.

Putting aside the objections in the previous paragraph, there is still one remaining problem. Let us assume, for the sake of argument, the respondents are only considering governmentally induced changes in income when making these assessments. Who should we predict a vote for if the respondent states that his financial status will improve in the next year, or next five years (during which time a second presidential election will have been held)? Lewis-Beck (1988a) argues that if the respondent expects improvement, we should predict a vote for the incumbent. In 1984, the year Lewis-Beck is examining, a respondent who believes his income is going to increase is predicted to vote for Reagan. What if this respondent believes his income will increase because of a Mondale victory? Lewis-Beck's model still predicts a vote for Reagan. Admittedly, this is not likely to be a problem in 1984, since 87 percent of those surveyed accurately predicted a Reagan victory (Lewis-Beck and Skalaban 1989). Of course, one could expect it to increase under either presidential candidate, but increase more under Mondale, further complicating matters. A close election, such as the 1960 presidential election, where less than 45 percent of those surveyed accurately forecast the outcome, might distort the analysis (Lewis-Beck and Skalaban 1989) or 2000 where 47 percent forecast a Bush victory and 51 percent forecast a Gore victory.[25] The theory might be correct, but this particular test of the hypothesis would likely fail to find supporting evidence of prospective voting.

One of the crucial assumptions I have made is that people actually do have expectations concerning the future of the economy and that these expectations are reasonably accurate.[26] Conover, Feldman, and Knight (1987) argue that people are not especially good at predicting changes in inflation and unemployment, and therefore prospective evaluations are necessarily flawed. Fortunately, however, the prospective model of voting behavior I examine here does not require voters to forecast the changes in direction of inflation or unemployment. All that is required is that voters anticipate which party, if either, would be better able to solve these problems or aid their personal financial situation. Conover, Feldman, and Knight (1987) also argue that because these prospective economic evaluations mention the parties' names, they are largely the result of partisan predispositions. MacKuen, Erikson, and Stimson (1989), however, point out that a rational expectations economist would argue that evaluations of the parties' abilities to solve problems are actual assessments rather than political biases.[27]

Miller and Wattenberg (1985) compare retrospective policy and performance voting in the presidential elections of 1952 through 1980. Although not specifically concerned with economic voting, this article shows that members of the electorate are capable of making the distinction between retrospective and prospective evaluations. Using open-ended items in the American National Election Studies (ANES), the authors find that people spontaneously offered judgments concerning the future performance of the parties. Lewis-Beck and Skalaban (1989) demonstrate that respondents are capable of forecasting the future concerning the outcome of presidential elections. The evidence fits with expectations. Landslide elections show a higher percentage of those surveyed predicting the outcome accurately than do close elections. Linden (1990) points out that consumers tend to be better predictors of upturns and downturns in the economy than are professional forecasters. Contrary to Key's (1966) assertion that forecasts are prohibitively hazy, it appears that voters not only forecast the future, but they are good at it. MacKuen, Erikson, and Stimson (1992, 606) state that "Understanding that expectations, rather than retrospections, lie at the core of political evaluations forces a new view of the political economy." This work attempts to take this new view explicitly into the area of voting behavior and economic evaluations.

Conclusion

This work will build on the economic voting literature in several ways. First, instead of looking at just a few election years, this work will look at elections from 1956 to 2000. We will be better able to discern if the model of voting behavior is generalizable across time. Are there conditions under which prospective voting is more likely? Second, and perhaps most important, when the data are available, the economic items used will both refer to the individual voter and the government's responsibility for the voter's economic condition. By using data of this nature, we can more directly test the hypothesis that voters are attempting to maximize their expected utility. When there is one item that refers to the person's financial situation without any attribution of responsibility and one item that has an attribution of responsibility to the government but is focused on the collective rather than the personal, I will make use of the latter. Third, by examining presidential, Senate, and House elections, we should be able to draw some conclusions about the nature of these various types of elections. We should also be able to make some comments on the role of separation of powers on the electoral process. Do voters respond to different stimuli in different types of elections? Fourth, by integrating models of voting behavior, we should have a more complete understanding of the role economics plays in influencing elections. Here is an outline of the chapters to follow:

Chapter 2 examines the bivariate relationship between these retrospective and prospective economic evaluations and presidential vote choice, as well as a simple economic model of presidential vote choice. Chapter 2 also presents the relationship between the retrospective and prospective economic items, so that we might assess the utility of differentiating between the two types of evaluations. Chapter 3 looks at the relationship between these economic evaluations and party identification. Chapter 4 returns to the question of vote choice. This chapter presents a more fully specified model of presidential vote choice. Alongside the retrospective and prospective economic items, the model includes several control variables, such as party identification and position on a liberal/conservative continuum. Additionally, this chapter presents a causal model of presidential vote choice. Chapter 5 largely replicates the analysis in chapter 4, with the dependent variable changed to House and then Senate vote choice, with an additional control: incumbency. Chapter 6 examines more closely the distinction between egocentric and sociotropic economic evaluations and their relevance for political decisions. Specifically, using the 1992 ANES we are able to address better what concerns voters. Are they concerned with themselves or are they concerned with the nation? Chapter 7 examines the question of whether we can forecast elections using expectations. This chapter draws in aggregate retrospective and prospective economic items, as well as various other items, to forecast presidential vote and seat change in the House and Senate. Chapter 8 brings together the findings from the earlier chapters and offers suggestions for future research.

Chapter 2

Simple Economic Relationships

In the first chapter, we looked, however briefly, at the differences between the extrapolative, adaptive, and rational expectations models of how people arrive at their forecasts of future events. If expectations are wholly, or substantially, predicted by past events, there is no need to look at expectations; earlier work on the retrospective voter would show the same findings as the tests of the prospective model. If the correlation between the retrospective and prospective items is one, or even comes very close to one, we would have little reason to progress with this investigation. If, however, the correlation between the retrospective and prospective evaluations is substantially less than one, there is reason for us to continue the investigation of prospective voting. While one should not expect the relationship between retrospections and prospections to be perfect, neither should one expect there to be no relationship between one's evaluations of the past and one's expectations of the parties' abilities in the future. It is not likely that people will throw away or ignore information concerning the past. No doubt, one's experience with the incumbent administration will play some role in helping one form expectations. In fact, it would be rather surprising if voters chose to ignore this information when forecasting. It would be similarly surprising if evaluations of the past were all the information one would take into account when making a forecast.

Table 2.1 presents the bivariate correlations between the retrospective and prospective economic evaluations during the presidential election years of 1956 through 2000. The reader should note that there is not an exact equivalence between the wording of the retrospective and prospective items. The retrospective items typically refer to the federal government, not a comparison of how one thinks each party would have performed. In contrast, the prospective items refer to both parties; the voters make a comparison between the parties. That aside, the relationship is in the expected

15

Table 2.1
A Bivariate Examination of the Relationship between Retrospective and Prospective Economic Evaluations: 1956–2000

	1956	1960	1964	1968	1972	1976	1980	1984	1988	1992	1996	2000
r	.28	.24	−.06	−.04#	.25	.44	−.49	.32	.19	.21	−.28	−.19
N	1473	1071	1149	897	889	1868	1449	1712	1612	2360	841	839

Note: Number sign (#) indicates insignificance at .05 level, 2-tailed. All the other correlations are significant at that level.

direction in every year. Given the coding of the items (higher values on the retrospective items mean the respondent thinks the incumbent party has done a good job, and higher values on the prospective items mean the respondent thinks the Republicans will do a better job), the relationship should be positive when the Republicans control the White House and negative when the Democrats control the White House.[1] The relationship between the retrospective and prospective items is significant in every year but one. The correlations, however, tell us that the relationship is far from perfect; the retrospective items do not wholly predict the prospective evaluations. In fact, in no year does the correlation between the retrospective and prospective items exceed .50, and in seven years the correlations are at or below .25. People are not completely ignoring the past, except perhaps in 1968, when deciding which party will provide for a more prosperous future. More important, they are not relying solely on their evaluations of the past performance of the incumbent administration when forecasting the future competence of the two parties.

To look more closely at the question of how much overlap there is between the retrospective and prospective items, we can examine the crosstabulation of the two items for 1992 in table 2.2a. Here we can see the relationship between the retrospective and prospective economic items more clearly. Those who believe Federal government has made their personal financial situation worse are likely to believe the Democratic Party is better able to provide a prosperous future. We should also note that just less than 50 percent of those seeing the Federal government as

Table 2.2a
Crosstabulations of Prospective and Retrospective
Economic Evaluations: 1992

Prospective	Retrospective			
	Worse	Same	Better	
Democrats	52.2%	32.9	26.8	
No difference	36.2%	44.3	30.5	
Republicans	11.6%	22.8	42.7	
N =	699	1579	82	2360

Note: The original coding of the retrospective item was from 1 = much worse to 5 = much better. For the purposes of this crosstabulation, I have recoded the item so that the two negative evaluations are collapsed into one score and the two positive evaluations are collapsed into one score.

having performed poorly either see no difference between the parties or believe the Republican Party, the incumbent party, will be better able to provide prosperity than would the Democratic Party. When we turn to the other side, we see that a strong plurality of those who believe the Federal government has made their personal financial situation better also believe the Republican Party is better able to provide prosperity in the future. Still, over one-quarter of the people who believe the Federal government has helped their personal financial situation believe the Democratic Party is better able to provide prosperity in the future, and almost one-third see no difference between the two parties' relative abilities to provide for a prosperous future. Taking these later two positions together, we can see that over one-half of those who believe that the Federal government has helped their financial position do not believe the Republican Party is better able than the Democratic Party to provide a prosperous future: they either are uncertain or believe the Democratic Party is better. To show that the year 1992 is not an anomaly, the analysis is repeated for 1996 in table 2.2b. Here again, the analysis shows us that the expected relationship between the retrospective and prospective items is present. Of those who believe that the Federal government has made their personal financial situation better, 55 percent believe the Democrats, the incumbent party, are better able than the Republicans to provide a prosperous future. Similarly, of those who believe that the Federal government has made their personal financial situation worse, just less than one-half think the Republican Party will be able to provide a more prosperous

Table 2.2b
Crosstabulations of Prospective
and Retrospective Economic Evaluations: 1996

	Retrospective			
Prospective	Worse	Same	Better	
Democrats	18.5%	26.2	55.0	
No difference	32.9%	42.8	26.5	
Republicans	48.6%	31.0	18.5	
N =	146	484	211	841

Note The original coding of the retrospective item was from 1= much worse to 5 = much better. For the purposes of this crosstabulation, I have recoded the item so that the two negative evaluations are collapsed into one score and the two positive evaluations are collapsed into one score.

future than would the Democrats. Here again, we should note that while a majority of those who thought the Federal government had helped their personal financial situation thought the Democratic Party would be better than the Republicans at providing prosperity in the future, 45 percent either saw no difference between the parties or thought the Republicans would be better able to provide prosperity. Clearly, one can be of the opinion that the incumbent party has done a good job without necessarily thinking they will do a good job in the future or that they will do better than the opposition. Similarly, when we turn to the other extreme, we can see in table 2.2b that of those who thought the Federal government had done a bad job, less than one-half stated that the Republicans could do a better job than the Democratic Party. Neither perceptions of success or failure necessarily carry over to perceptions of the parties' abilities to provide for a prosperous future. Note that these are the two most recent years with an incumbent seeking re-election. Here is where we should expect to see the strongest relationship between the retrospective and prospective economic items. Tables 2.1, 2.2a, and 2.2b show us that the anticipated relationship between the retrospective and prospective items is present, but these tables also show us that retrospective evaluations do not, by any stretch of the imagination, determine the respondents' prospective evaluations. At least at first empirical blush, the theoretical distinction between retrospective and prospective items is supported by an examination of the data.

The results in tables 2.1, 2.2a, and 2.2b show us that the extrapolative model of expectation formation is not a terribly good explanation of how people forecast the future. If the extrapolative model were an accurate description of how people made forecasts, we would have seen in table 2.2a, for example, 100 percent in each cell along the diagonal starting in the upper left corner. Everyone who responded that the Federal government made things worse would have predicted the Democratic Party to be better than the Republican Party. Everyone who saw the Federal government as having had no influence on the financial well-being would have seen no difference between the two parties. Finally, everyone who saw the Federal government as having a positive influence on their financial well-being would have responded that the Republican Party would be better than the Democratic Party.[2] It, however, does not allow us to test as cleanly the distinction between adaptive and rational expectations. We do not know what each cell of each of the tables should look like under these two models of expectation formation. One would think that since the adaptive expectations model holds that we only modify our previous forecasts by our errors, the predictive ability of the retrospective evaluations should be quite high if it is an accurate description of how we forecast the future. As the predictive ability of the retrospective evaluations is not terribly strong, we have reason to at least doubt the verisimilitude of the adaptive expectations approach. By the elimination of alternative models of expectation formation, one can argue that the results in tables 2.1, 2.2a, and 2.2b support, or are at least consistent with, the rational expectations model. Most important, for this work, it is clear that retrospective and prospective evaluations are not identical, or even near identical. As long as one agrees with the contention that retrospective and prospective evaluations are theoretically and empirically distinct, regardless of whether one thinks that people develop their expectations through the process described by the rational expectations approach, there is reason to go forward with this examination.

We can see that there are differences between the retrospective and prospective economic evaluations. Is this distinction important? The next step is to assess the relationship between these retrospective and prospective economic items and vote choice. Is there anything worthy of further investigation? As presidential elections have been the mainstay of research on voting behavior, they are a reasonable place to begin this investigation. It is the office of the president for which we expect, or perhaps hope, the electorate to hold candidates accountable. The presidency is the focal point of government and the campaign for the office lasts for what many people consider an interminably long time (at least in recent years). If we do not see a strong relationship between the prospective evaluations and presidential vote in a simple model of vote choice, then we have little hope of seeing such a relationship in a more fully specified model of presidential voting or for lower level offices.

If the prospective model of voting behavior holds true and voters do hold candidates accountable, we have reason to believe that presidential elections do produce a mandate of sorts (Miller and Wattenberg 1985). While the retrospective model calls for simply a ratification or rejection of the incumbent party, the prospective model calls upon the voters to select from more than one party. The implication is that voters are making a statement concerning the direction the government should take. This statement should not be taken too strongly. Voters are, for the most part, selecting from two candidates. They may actually dislike both candidates, but dislike one more than the other. As Key (1966) put it years ago, if voters are given a choice between two rascals, a rascal will most certainly win. Many observers have argued that voters are often not selecting a candidate with whom they are enthralled, but rather they are selecting what they perceive to be the lesser of two evils. The candidate who gets votes in this fashion cannot be said to have the ringing endorsement of the electorate. All we can say with some degree of confidence is that the voters appear to have preferred one candidate to the other.[3] In short, the prospective model of voting does not argue that voters are casting ballots for their most preferred candidate out of a large pool of candidates, but rather they are selecting the candidate that is most preferred, or disliked least, from the candidates on the ballot. Here, for simplicity sake, we only consider the major party contenders. Nonetheless, if the prospective model is an accurate description of voting behavior, it does imply that voters are more sophisticated than the retrospective model would lead us to believe. Of the two models, the prospective model offers the greater opportunity for the voters to hold candidates accountable and to confer a mandate, albeit a hazy one.

How strongly do the retrospective and prospective evaluations relate to vote choice in presidential elections? As we can see in table 2.3 with the bivariate correlations between these evaluations and vote choice, the prospective items are quite strongly related to vote choice.[4] In fact, it would appear as though they are stronger than the retrospective items. We can, however, note one reversal of this pattern when we turn to the non-economic retrospective and prospective items: attitudes toward Carter's handling of the hostage crisis in Iran (RIRAN) are more strongly related to vote choice than are expectations of which party is better able to keep the United States out of war (Pwar). The prospective economic items appear to be consistently more powerful than are their retrospective counterparts. The findings, at this point, if nothing else, give us reason to proceed with the investigation of prospective evaluations and their influence on vote choice.

So that the reader can get a better sense of the relationship between these retrospective and prospective items and vote choice, tables 2.4a and 2.4b present the crosstabulation of presidential vote choice and the retrospective and prospective economic items for the 1992 and 1996 presidential elections.

As one can see in tables 2.4a and 2.4b, both the retrospective and prospective items do a reasonably good job of discriminating among voters. First, we look at 1992. Among those who thought the national government had made their financial situation much worse, just less than 85 percent voted against George Bush.[5] Among those who thought the government had made their financial situation much better, just less than 85 percent voted for George Bush's reelection. Looking at the full array of responses to the retrospective economic item, there is a monotonic relationship between the economic item and vote choice. Among those who thought that the Federal government had made their financial situation somewhat worse, just over 70 percent voted against George Bush. Among those who thought the national government had helped their personal financial situation somewhat, two-thirds supported George Bush. While the retrospective economic item does a good job of discriminating among voters, a look at the bottom of table 2.4a shows that the prospective items do

Table 2.3
Bivariate Relationships between Presidential Vote Choice and Retrospective and Prospective Evaluations

	1956	1960	1964	1968	1972	1976	1980	1984	1988	1992	1996	2000
RWAR	.37											
WORLD		.28	−.22									
RIRAN							−.53					
RPOS								.40	.29	.30	−.43	−.38
FAFFAIRS											.57	
PWAR	.60	.63	.59				.51	.61	.55	.49		.47
RETRO	.23	.22	−.08	−.17								
RGOV					.42	.44	−.55	.35	.25	.25	−.34	
RPROB												−.22
PROSP	.51	.50	.45	.47	.48							
PGOV						.64	.66					
PECON										.73	.64	
PPROB								.68	.61		.61	.65

Note: All items are significant at the .05 level, 2-tailed or better.

Table 2.4a

Crosstabulations of Presidential Vote Choice
and Retrospective and Prospective Evaluations: 1992

Federal Government's Influence on Respondent's Financial Well-Being

	Much Worse	Somewhat Worse	No Difference	Somewhat Better	Much Better
Clinton	84.6%	70.5	53.0	33.3	16.7
Bush	15.4%	29.5	47.0	66.7	83.3
N =	123	281	885	39	12	1340

Which Party Would Be Better for the Nation's Financial Well-Being?

	Democrat	No Difference	Republicans
Clinton	96.4%	49.3	6.3
Bush	3.6%	50.7	93.8
N =	554	458	320	1332

Table 2.4b

Crosstabulations of Presidential Vote Choice
and Retrospective and Prospective Evaluations: 1996

Federal Government's Influence on Respondent's Financial Well-Being

	Much Worse	Somewhat Worse	No Difference	Somewhat Better	Much Better
Clinton	36.8%	28.7	53.6	81.5	93.8
Dole	63.2%	71.3	46.4	18.5	6.3
N =	38	129	549	260	32
					1008

Which Party Would Be Better for the Nation's Financial Well−Being

	Democrat	No Difference	Republicans
Clinton	93.5%	71.4	18.4
Dole	6.5%	28.6	81.6
N =	186	161	190
			537

a better job. Of those who thought the Democrats would do a better job in managing the nation's economy, more than 95 percent voted for Bill Clinton. Among those who thought the Republican Party would do a better job, just less than 95 percent voted for George Bush. Those in the middle split almost evenly between Bush and Clinton.

When we turn to 1996, we see that these items discriminate among voters in a similar fashion. With the retrospective item, we see that the better off the respondents felt, the more likely they were to support Clinton. The only violation of monotonicity is the shift from much worse to somewhat worse. Clinton does better among those who believe the Federal government has made their financial situation much worse than he does among those who believe that the Federal government has made their financial situation somewhat worse. He receives the votes of approximately one-third of those who believe the Federal government has made their financial situation much worse and approximately 28 percent of the vote of those who believe the Federal government has made their financial situation somewhat worse. Still, he does not do particularly well with either group.[6] If we look at the prospective item from 1996, we see that it again appears to discriminate between the candidates more clearly than does the retrospective item. There are, however, two items aside from the expected relationship between the prospective item and vote that stand out. First, Clinton does remarkably well among those who see no difference between the parties; he gets over 70 percent of the vote of this group. Second, he gets almost 20 percent of the vote of those who believe the Republican party can better provide economic prosperity. Most important, as is shown in tables 2.4a and 2.4b, is that both the retrospective and prospective economic evaluations are related to the behavior of voters in presidential elections.

Knowing that there is some relationship between these retrospective and prospective items and also knowing that there is likely to be some shared variance in the explanation of vote choice, one should do more than examine the relationship between each type of evaluation and vote choice in isolation. What happens when we put these retrospective and prospective economic items in a single logistic regression equation predicting presidential vote choice?[7] Do both types of evaluations have an influence on voting behavior? Table 2.5 presents the results of this analysis for the years 1956 through 2000. The first observation is that both the retrospective and prospective items are statistically significant in virtually every year examined. The prospective items are significant in every year and the retrospective items are significant except for 1960 and 1964. Additionally, the equations have reasonably good explanatory power in each year examined. One should note, however, that the R-square improves considerably in 1972, just as the retrospective items have an explicit reference to government. Furthermore, in 1976, the R-square increases again. The reader

Table 2.5
A Multivariate Comparison of Retrospective and Prospective Economic Evaluations on Presidential Vote Choice: 1956–2000

	1956	1960	1964	1968	1972	1976	1980	1984	1988	1992	1996	2000
RETRO	.27*	−.03	−.05	−.47*								
RGOV					1.47*	.61*	−.33*	.66*	.58*	.37*	−.67*	
RPROB												−.44*
PROSP	1.14*	1.28*	1.26*	1.12*	1.75*							
PGOV						1.69*	1.40*					
PPROB								2.56*	2.63*			2.48*
PECON										2.95*	2.08*	
CONST	−3.34	−3.57	−4.15	−2.17	−5.57	−8.54	−4.11	−6.71	−6.75	−4.00	−2.88	−4.37
R²	.22	.21	.18	.21	.29	.41	.44	.42	.35	.47	.38	.37
N	1086	775	830	606	641	1138	651	1243	1119	1318	525	541

Note: Asterisk (*) indicates significance at .05 level, 2-tailed or better.

should note that it is in this year that the prospective evaluations start referring to the nation's rather than the individual's financial well-being. We shall return to this distinction later (chapter 6). The important point is that these retrospective and prospective items are significant across the board, regardless of the changes in how the questions are worded.

How much influence do these items have on voting behavior? Are they consequential? One way of assessing these variables is to treat the equation as a probability model.[8] Let us first look at 1992. An individual who is completely neutral on the question of the Democratic and Republican parties' ability to provide a prosperous future and who also thinks the national government has neither made their personal financial situation better nor worse has a .51 probability of voting for George Bush. If we have a similarly situated individual who instead thinks the national government has made his personal financial situation much worse, this person has a .34 probability of voting for George Bush. Now let us turn to someone who is neutral about the past performance of the federal government but believes the Republican Party is better able to provide for a prosperous future. This person has a .95 probability of voting for George Bush. Again, a similarly situated individual except for thinking the Democratic Party is better able to provide for a prosperous future has a .95 probability of voting for Bill Clinton. Clearly, changes in one's estimation of the parties' abilities to provide a prosperous future influence vote choice. Let us now turn to 1996. Here, let us hone in on the prospective item. Someone who is neutral on the retrospective item and believes that the Republican Party is better able to provide a prosperous future has a high probability (.79) of supporting Bob Dole. Similarly, one who is neutral about the past but positive about the Democrats' ability to provide for a prosperous future is virtually certain (.94) to support Bill Clinton for reelection.[9] The reader can do similar calculations for the earlier years and arrive at similar conclusions. Suffice it to say, these economic evaluations at least have the potential to be a powerful influence on voting behavior. Furthermore, it certainly looks as though the prospective items have a greater ability to influence voting behavior than do the retrospective items. Later (chapter 4), we will examine a more fully specified model of presidential vote choice in which we can examine the relative power of a host of variables.

While looking at these logistic regression equations is very useful, it might make the presentation more clear to show crosstabulations that indicate how strong the prospective items are when the retrospective evaluations are taken into account. Tables 2.6a and 2.6b show us that relationship. Again, we first look at 1992. Regardless of which category of the retrospective item one places oneself, the prospective item discriminates similarly. No matter the respondents' views concerning the past performance of the

Table 2.6a
Crosstabulations of Presidential Vote Choice
by Prospective Economic Evaluations
Controlling for Retrospective Economic Evaluations: 1992

Retrospective Worse

Which Party Would Be Better for the Nation's Financial Well-Being?

	Democrat	No Difference	Republicans	
Clinton	96.2%	57.4	10.4	
Bush	3.8%	42.6	89.6	
N =	236	115	48	399

Retrospective Same

Which Party Would Be Better for the Nation's Financial Well-Being?

	Democrat	No Difference	Republicans	
Clinton	96.4%	47.6	6.3	
Bush	3.6%	52.4	93.8	
N =	302	328	240	870

Retrospective Better

Which Party Would Be Better for the Nation's Financial Well-Being

	Democrat	No Difference	Republicans	
Clinton	100.0%	33.3	0.0	
Bush	0.0%	66.7	100.0	
N =	11	12	26	49

Note: The original coding of the retrospective item was from 1 = much worse to 5 = much better. For the purposes of this crosstabulation, I have recoded the item so that the two negative evaluations are collapsed into one score and the two positive evaluations are collapsed into one score.

Table 2.6b
Crosstabulations of Presidential Vote Choice
by Prospective Economic Evaluations
Controlling for Retrospective Economic Evaluations: 1996

Retrospective Worse
Which Party Would Be Better for the Nation's Financial Well-Being?

	Democrat	No Difference	Republicans	
Clinton	93.8%	59.1	5.7	
Dole	6.2%	40.9	94.3	
N =	16	22	53	91

Retrospective Same
Which Party Would Be Better for the Nation's Financial Well-Being?

	Democrat	No Difference	Republicans	
Clinton	90.8%	69.1	18.6	
Dole	9.2%	30.9	81.4	
N =	76	97	102	275

Retrospective Better
Which Party Would Be Better for the Nation's Financial Well-Being?

	Democrat	No Difference	Republicans	
Clinton	95.5%	89.2	39.4	
Dole	4.5%	10.8	60.6	
N =	89	37	33	159

Note: The original coding of the retrospective item was from 1 = much worse to 5 = much better. For the purposes of this crosstabulation, I have recoded the item so that the two negative evaluations are collapsed into one score and the two positive evaluations are collapsed into one score.

Federal government, more than 95 percent of those who viewed the Democratic Party as better able to provide a prosperous future supported Bill Clinton. Similarly, regardless of the retrospective evaluations, more than 89 percent of those who viewed the Republican Party as better able to provide a prosperous future supported George Bush.

Looking at those who see no difference between the two parties' abilities to provide for a prosperous future, we can also see that the retrospective items have an influence. Among this group, a distinct pattern is present. Those who hold negative evaluations of the national government's performance are most likely to have voted against George Bush. Those who hold a positive view of the national government's past performance are those most likely to have voted for George Bush. Clearly, both of these retrospective and prospective evaluations have the potential to influence the decisions of voters. Looking down the center column shows those voters who see no difference between the two parties' abilities to provide a prosperous future. We can see from an inspection of this center column that the retrospective item does discriminate well. As evaluations of the past performance of the incumbent administration improve, the percentage supporting George Bush goes up.

When we turn to 1996, we see much the same picture as we did for 1992, but there are some intriguing differences that should be noted momentarily. Let us, however, first note the similarities. The prospective item tends to discriminate among the voters rather well. Regardless of the retrospective evaluation, over 90 percent of those who believe that the Democratic Party is better able to provide economic prosperity than is the Republican Party supported Bill Clinton. As one would expect, among those who are neutral concerning the parties' relative abilities to provide for a prosperous future, the retrospective item does help to explain the choices made by the voters. The prospective item also works much as one would expect on the Republican side. Regardless of one's evaluation of the past performance of the incumbent administration, those who view the Republican Party as being better able than the Democrats to provide for a prosperous future are very likely to vote for Bob Dole. It is interesting to note that Bill Clinton does remarkably well among those who believe that the Federal government has done a good job but the Republicans would be better than the Democrats at providing a prosperous economic future. Clinton gets just under 40 percent of the vote of this group. In contrast, in 1992, of those who viewed the Federal government as having performed well but thought the Democratic party would do a better job, Bush got no votes. Perhaps Clinton's skills as a politician explain the rather dramatic difference between these two candidates.

To this point, I have largely ignored one problem. I have not said much about the different items the ANES uses across the years to get at the questions of the government's management of the economy and the parties' respective abilities to provide for a prosperous future. As we well know from the lengthy debate over the level of ideological thinking on the part of the electorate (Brunk 1978; Nie and Anderson 1974; Nie and Rabjohn 1979; Sullivan, Pierson, and Marcus 1978), using different questions to get a topic over time is at best controversial, at worst wrongheaded. We can take some solace in noting that the same survey items when possible are employed over time. As one cannot go back in time and change the items in the ANESs of the past, one can only make use of what is available. We can look at the results of the analysis to determine if the break points accompany a change in the survey items used, as I have done already. If a shift in the way in which we think the electorate views politics accompanies a shift in the survey item used, we should at least be cautious in our interpretations. One can easily argue that it is the change in question wording that is being reflected in the results, rather than a change in the way in which the electorate views politics. To make the best of an admittedly bad situation, if the findings of the analysis are largely the same across different survey items, we at least have some confidence that our interpretations are not dependent on one particular survey item.

While there are the general problems of using different survey items across time, this work has to make do with some very specific survey item changes that are worthy of some discussion. First, the prospective economic items change over time. From 1956 through 1972, the ANES asks one particular question of the respondents. The ANES specifically asks the respondents which party, if either, will be better for their personal finances in the future. After 1972 for the most part, the ANES asks questions that refer to the nation's economy. The distinction between one's personal economic well-being and the nation's well-being is an important one. Kinder and Kiewiet (1979, 1981) argue that voters are more likely to take the nation's well-being into account than their own well-being. If we note a change in economic voting immediately after 1972, we should be somewhat cautious in making any broad generalizations. Miller and Wattenberg (1985) argue that these collective items are significant, not because they refer to the nation, but rather because they reference the political parties. Lane (1986, 316) argues that these sociotropic items are particularly ambiguous. He offers several possible interpretations of these items. First, unable to see the personal effects of public policy, citizens may use national news as evidence of their personal well-being. Second, people see that there are collective goods, such as low inflation and unemployment, that they cannot have without others benefitting similarly. Their self-interest is served by policies that benefit others. Third, the degree to which others are well-off affects the probability that the self will be well-off. Fourth, these sociotropic items may reflect some sense of altruism. We should note that Kinder and Kiewiet (1981) make the point that sociotropic voting does not necessarily mean altruistic voting. Suffice it to say, there are a variety of possible interpretations of these sociotropic/mediated economic items.

While there are several possible interpretations of these sociotropic items, I, not surprisingly given the theoretical framework within which I am presenting this material, do not agree with the argument that these items are simply tapping into an other regarding nature of the electorate. Instead, I argue that voters look upon the economy as a collective good to some extent. A voter, for example, cannot get the benefit of a low inflation rate without others getting the same low inflation rate. So if a voter casts a ballot for a party that the voter believes will help to bring about a low rate of inflation, the voter is not acting in such a fashion to help others. Rather, the voter is looking out for their own interests. The nice thing is that when a voter acts in such a fashion, it works to everyone's advantage.

Instead of voting on the basis of these items being indivisible collective goods, voters may be using these collective evaluations as a diagnostic tool. While it may be difficult to ascertain the effect of the national government on one's economic well-being, the state of the national economy might give us some guidance as to the effects of the government on our individual well-being. If, for example, a voter's personal financial situation has gotten worse but the nation's economy is booming, the voter might not be inclined to blame the government for the voter doing poorly. Similarly, if the national economy is doing poorly but the voter is doing well, the voter might be of the opinion that the national government has hindered the voter's prospects, no matter how well the voter is doing at the present time. Consequently, a voter who is doing well financially might well vote against the incumbent party because the voter thinks the incumbent party has not done as well as it should have. Chapter 6 has a more thorough investigation of this question.

Conclusion

This chapter addresses two major questions. First, is there a distinction worthy of investigation? That is, are retrospective and prospective evaluations sufficiently different that we can learn something about voting behavior that we would not know by only examining one. Clearly, the evidence is on the side that urges us forward. While there is some relationship between retrospective and prospective evaluations, they are by no means synonymous. Second, are these prospective evaluations related to vote choice? Again, the evidence points us consistently in the same direction, regardless of the election year or the particular survey item employed. At a minimum, the evidence suggests that we should look more closely at the question of whether voters pay attention to the future when casting their ballots or making political evaluations.

Appendix 2.1
Prospective Evaluations:
Are They Partisan Rationalizations?

One other concern that one might have is that these prospective evaluations are little more than partisan rationalizations.[10] In the fashion envisioned by the authors of *The American Voter*, one uses party identification to filter information about the political world. If one is a Democrat (Republican), all that is good is the result of the efforts of the Democratic (Republican) Party. All that is bad is either the result of the nefarious activities of the Republican (Democratic) Party or the result of random events that are not under the control of the party with which one identifies. Later chapters in the book consider this issue in some detail. Nonetheless, it is important to at least look at some simple relationships before going further. If these prospective evaluations are wholly or largely determined by party identification, we again would have little reason to proceed. We should expect some relationship between the two items, especially, as is argued later in this work, since party identification is partly the result of prospective evaluations. What we can do for the entirety of the years studied is simply look at the simple regression of the prospective items on party identification and the associated retrospective items. This is shown in table 2.7.

We can see that there is the anticipated relationship between the prospective items and party identification. Looking across the years, we can also see that party identification and the associated retrospective item do not explain much of the prospective items. In no year does the R-square associated with any of these equations reach .50. In fact, in no year does the R-square reach .40. In just over one-half the equations, the R-square is below .25. If we look at the non-presidential election years, the picture is even more supportive of the argument that these items are not simply partisan rationalizations.

Table 2.7
Prospective Economic Evaluations as a Function
of Party Identification and Retrospective Evaluations: 1956–2000

	1956	1960	1964	1968	1972	1976	1980	1984	1988	1992	1996	2000
RETRO	.38	.33	−.12	−.04#								
RGOV					.18	.35	−.17	.18	.10	.12	−.15	
RPROB												.13
PID	.58	.52	.59	.61	.32	.67	.61	.40	.38	.56	.55	.49
R^2	.24	.22	.20	.18	.21	.37	.37	.28	.24	.38	.38	.30
N	1428	976	1134	887	878	1861	1137	1691	1536	2332	834	827

Note: Number sign (#) indicates insignificance at .05 level, 2-tailed. All the other coefficients are significant at that level.

Chapter 3

Party Identification
Is It Changeable? Is It Explicable?

Over the past forty-plus years, political scientists have conducted much research on the stability of party identification.[1] Campbell et al. (1960), in *The American Voter*, argue that party identification is largely stable; only 20 percent of those surveyed report changing their party identification at any point in their lifetimes. Hyman (1959), Greenstein (1965), and Niemi and Jennings (1991) argue that party identification is acquired in childhood, well before the acquisition of any substantive political information. If party identification is as stable as the authors of *The American Voter* strongly suggest and it is acquired before any substantive knowledge of politics is acquired as Hyman and others would argue, it would suggest that the political parties have little reason to pay attention to the attitudes of the electorate. Regardless of the actions of the political parties, they will have roughly the same number of adherents, assuming new people entering the political world split the same way the current electorate has divided.

Since party identification has been viewed as a long-term, stable attitude and it has been found to be highly correlated with vote choice, it has been almost required as a control variable in models of vote choice. If the other variables show themselves to be significant when placed alongside party identification, then and only then can we say they are in fact a significant influence on vote choice. Without the inclusion of party identification, findings concerning other variables are considered suspect, at best. Indeed, party identification is included as a control variable in virtually every model of vote choice that I can recall seeing in the political science journals.[2] Yet, if party identification is changeable and it changes in response to the other variables in our equations explaining vote choice, we will necessarily understate the importance of the other explanatory variables. Power that should be attributed to the other items in the equations will be assigned, inaccurately, to party identification. We may still, in the interest of caution, want to include party identification as an independent variable in our models of voting behavior. We should, however, recognize that this caution will make it more likely that we will reject hypotheses concerning theories we are testing. This caution might serve the purpose of helping to persuade those who think that party identification is stable.

The authors of *The American Voter* based their argument concerning the stability of party identification on the ability of the survey respondents to recall accurately whether they had changed their partisanship. As Niemi, Katz, and Newman (1980) have shown, the ability of survey respondents to accurately recall past behavior is not terribly high. Fortunately for us, after the publication of *The American Voter*, the American National Election Study panel surveys of 1956–1960, 1972–1976, 1980, and 1990–1992 became available. These panel studies, in which the same people are repeatedly surveyed, make it possible for us to ascertain the extent to which party identification changes over a relatively short period. Moreover, by making use of panel surveys over such a long time, we will be more certain that the findings are not simply the result of period effects. If the findings are consistent over the entire set of panel surveys, we will have greater confidence that they are generalizable than if we had simply relied upon a single panel survey.

Contrary to the picture of lifelong stability, we can see that party identification, while reasonably stable, is changeable.[3] Correlations of party identification in one wave with party identification in another wave presents a picture of high stability, though not rigidity. The typical tau-b correlation is in the .70s.[4] This correlational analysis, of course, ignores shifts that are global. If every individual in the survey moved one position toward the Democratic Party, the correlation between wave one and wave two party identification will be 1.00.[5] One's previous position will perfectly predict one's current position. Using correlation coefficients to estimate the level of change will understate the amount of change, if there is movement that is largely in one direction, as there typically was in each of the panel studies, rather than compensating changes in each direction. It may somewhat more instructive to look at the actual level of change.

Table 3.1 shows the level of stability of the 7-point scale of party identification from one wave to another. While there is a great deal of stability, we should not ignore the change that is also readily apparent. If one looks down the diagonal from the upper left at the numbers in bold, one can see that a plurality stay in exactly the same position from one wave to the next. Yet, we can also see that some change is occurring. For example from 1956 to 1958, almost 23 percent of the strong Democrats left their position. Similarly, during this same time, over 40 percent of the strong Republicans left

Table 3.1
Changes in Partisanship on the 7-Point Scale

1956–1958

	Strong Dem	Not Very Strong	Ind-Dem	Ind	Ind-Rep	Not Very Strong	Strong Rep	
Strong Dem	77.2	34.3	17.6	6.5	3.1	1.9	3.0	
Not Very Strong	19.4	54.7	35.1	15.1	10.3	8.1	2.4	
Ind-Dem	0.9	6.9	32.4	11.8	10.3	1.9	0.6	
Ind	0.4	2.0	8.1	39.8	15.5	5.0	0.6	
Ind-Rep	0.0	0.0	0.0	16.1	24.7	8.1	5.3	
Not Very Strong	0.4	2.0	5.4	7.5	23.7	58.1	29.0	
Strong Rep	1.7	0.0	1.4	3.2	12.4	16.9	59.2	
N =	232	245	74	93	97	160	169	1070

1958–1960

	Strong Dem	Not Very Strong	Ind-Dem	Ind	Ind-Rep	Not Very Strong	Strong Rep	
Strong Dem	67.1	23.7	9.3	8.3	0.0	2.2	1.2	
Not Very Strong	26.9	57.5	29.1	11.5	10.5	2.6	1.2	
Ind-Dem	1.7	8.1	30.2	8.3	7.9	0.4	0.0	
Ind	2.3	4.5	18.6	46.9	15.8	4.8	1.2	
Ind-Rep	0.6	2.6	10.5	15.6	31.6	12.3	5.9	
Not Very Strong	0.8	2.9	2.3	8.3	22.4	52.9	21.8	
Strong Rep	0.6	0.6	0.0	1.0	11.8	24.7	68.8	
N =	353	308	86	96	76	227	170	1316

(*continued*)

Table 3.1
(continued)

1972–1974

	Strong Dem	Not Very Strong	Ind-Dem	Ind	Ind-Rep	Not Very Strong	Strong Rep	
Strong Dem	**66.7**	26.0	11.5	6.7	3.4	2.7	1.6	
Not Very Strong	23.0	**49.8**	21.9	8.4	6.8	6.3	2.1	
Ind-Dem	6.3	12.6	**49.2**	20.2	7.9	1.8	2.1	
Ind	2.3	6.4	13.7	**47.2**	18.6	9.4	4.8	
Ind-Rep	0.9	3.0	3.3	10.7	**35.6**	17.5	5.8	
Not Very Strong	0.9	1.5	0.5	5.6	19.8	**46.6**	28.0	
Strong Rep	0.0	0.7	0.0	1.1	7.9	15.7	**55.6**	
N =	222	404	183	178	177	223	189	1576

1974–1976

	Strong Dem	Not Very Strong	Ind-Dem	Ind	Ind-Rep	Not Very Strong	Strong Rep	
Strong Dem	**62.5**	17.0	9.3	2.4	0.0	1.8	0.0	
Not Very Strong	27.8	**57.8**	22.5	8.7	6.2	1.3	1.3	
Ind-Dem	4.9	12.2	**42.6**	14.9	4.1	1.3	0.6	
Ind	1.4	4.6	11.8	**48.6**	15.8	6.3	2.6	
Ind-Rep	1.7	3.6	8.8	18.3	**41.8**	16.6	5.2	
Not Very Strong	1.7	4.6	3.9	5.8	23.3	**55.2**	30.3	
Strong Rep	0.0	0.3	1.0	1.4	8.9	17.5	**60.0**	
N =	288	329	204	208	146	223	155	1553

(continued)

Table 3.1
(*continued*)

1980 Wave 1–1980 Wave 3

	Strong Dem	Not Very Strong	Ind-Dem	Ind	Ind-Rep	Not Very Strong	Strong Rep	
Strong Dem	**71.5**	16.8	3.9	1.0	1.2	0.0	0.0	
Not Very Strong	25.4	**61.8**	27.3	16.3	9.9	1.5	0.0	
Ind-Dem	2.3	9.2	**41.6**	15.4	9.9	0.8	0.0	
Ind	0.0	5.2	15.6	**41.3**	7.5	6.0	1.7	
Ind-Rep	0.8	2.9	9.1	15.4	**50.6**	11.3	1.7	
Not Very Strong	0.0	2.9	2.6	9.6	17.3	**62.4**	16.7	
Strong Rep	0.0	1.2	0.0	1.0	3.7	18.0	**80.0**	
N=	130	173	77	104	81	133	60	758

1990–1992

	Strong Dem	Not Very Strong	Ind-Dem	Ind	Ind-Rep	Not Very Strong	Strong Rep	
Strong Dem	**65.9**	20.2	9.0	5.2	1.8	1.9	1.7	
Not Very Strong	20.7	**43.9**	27.1	4.3	4.2	2.4	0.0	
Ind-Dem	7.2	20.6	**38.0**	15.5	15.6	4.3	1.7	
Ind	2.2	6.1	10.8	**46.6**	16.8	6.7	2.5	
Ind-Rep	1.1	4.2	7.2	13.8	**38.3**	13.5	6.6	
Not Very Strong	1.4	2.3	5.4	12.9	16.8	**53.8**	21.5	
Strong Rep	1.4	2.7	2.4	1.7	6.6	17.3	**66.1**	
N =	276	262	166	116	167	208	121	1316

their position. When one looks at the intermediate positions, the degree of volatility is even higher. Of course, we should note that those in the intermediate positions have two directions in which they can move. Those at the extremes can only move in one direction—toward the other party. Those at the extremes who become more ardent supporters of their party have no stronger location than where they placed themselves earlier. The other time periods show roughly the same picture, while party identification is reasonably stable, it is not rigid. This lack of rigidity is not a result of only examining more volatile periods, such as the early 1970s or 1980. During even the allegedly placid 1950s, party identification was changeable.

One might argue that the changes we see in table 3.1 are the result of using the 7-point scale of party identification. If, however, we were to look at the 3-point scale (Democrat, Independent, Republican), one might expect the picture to be much different. Looking at table 3.2, we can see that this is most definitely not the case. Yes, party identification does appear to be more stable, but we should keep in mind a movement of one position is now much more monumental. With the 7-point scale, a movement of one position might mean only a change in strength without actually leaving one's party identification. Here, a movement of one position means either leaving one's party identification for political independence or leaving political independence for identification with a political party. Movement of two positions means changing from one party identification to the other. Nonetheless, we do see movement. Again, the stable position is represented by the diagonal running from the upper left to the lower right. We see from 1956 to 1958 over 7 percent of the Democrats left their party and over 18 percent of the Republicans left their party. Again, this pattern is very similar for the other years under investigation. Like the 7-point scale, the 3-point scale shows some volatility. Between 1956 and 1958, almost 8 percent of the Republicans became Democrats. Just over 2 percent of the Democrats became Republicans between these years.

Showing that there is change is one thing; being able to explain that change is another. If this change is anything more than random fluctuation, we should be able to explain it. We should note that the aggregate patterns fit with expectations.[6] The late 1950s (with a recession) and the early 1970s (with the advent of stagflation and Watergate) were not good years for the Republican Party. The bulk of the movement for these years is toward the Democratic Party. Similarly, 1980 (with a recession, the Iranian hostage crisis, and the Soviet invasion of Afghanistan) was not a good year for the Democratic Party. The bulk of the movement for this year is toward the Republican Party. Change from 1990 to 1992 is much more balanced. Scholars, noting the apparent volatility of party identification, have attempted to explain the changes that take place. Fiorina (1981a) finds that changes in partisanship can be directly attributed to retrospective evaluations.[7] Fiorina's (1981a) logic flows quite clearly from the work of V. O. Key. Key (1966) argued that voters either reward or punish the incumbent party in its bid for reelection. Fiorina argues that we are pulled toward or repelled by the incumbent party's past performance. Party identification starts out from socialization, but once we become adults and active, however minimally, in the political world, our party identification is based on our experiences. The impact of our parental socialization weakens the further we are from it. It is, in a sense, a running tally of our evaluations of the incumbent parties of our lifetimes. Although Fiorina (1981a) looked at both retrospective and prospective voting, he did not make the extension to party identification. Here, Fiorina only looked at the retrospective side.

Aside from the retrospective economic and prospective items discussed in the preceding chapter, there are other factors that one should include in a model of party identification. Briefly stated, events specific to the time and position along a liberal/conservative continuum may have an influence

Table 3.2
Changes in Partisanship on the 3-Point Scale

| | 1956–1958 | | | |
	Democrat	Independent	Republican	
Democrat	**92.7**	27.3	7.6	
Independent	5.2	**53.8**	10.6	
Republican	2.1	18.9	**81.8**	
N =	477	264	329	1070
	1958–1960			
	Democrat	Independent	Republican	
Democrat	**88.0**	23.3	3.8	
Independent	9.5	**62.4**	13.1	
Republican	2.4	14.3	**83.1**	
N =	661	258	397	1316

(*continued*)

Table 3.2
(continued)

1972–1974

	Democrat	Independent	Republican	
Democrat	80.7	19.7	6.6	
Independent	17.6	68.8	21.4	
Republican	1.8	11.5	72.1	
N =	626	538	412	1576

1974–1976

	Democrat	Independent	Republican	
Democrat	82.0	17.4	2.4	
Independent	14.6	69.7	17.7	
Republican	3.4	12.9	79.9	
N =	617	558	412	1553

1980 Wave 1–1980 Wave 3

	Democrat	Independent	Republican	
Democrat	86.5	19.5	1.0	
Independent	11.2	69.1	13.5	
Republican	2.3	11.5	85.5	
N =	303	262	193	758

1990–1992

	Democrat	Independent	Republican	
Democrat	75.7	18.0	3.3	
Independent	20.4	66.6	19.5	
Republican	3.9	15.4	77.2	
N =	538	449	329	1316

on party identification, as well as on voting behavior. Events specific to the time include such items as Gerald Ford's pardon of Richard Nixon. Since President Ford suffered a considerable drop in his approval ratings and the Republicans did so poorly in the House and Senate elections (losing 48 and 4 seats, respectively) after the 1974 resignation of Richard Nixon and Ford's subsequent pardon, it would be rather surprising if the Watergate scandal did not hurt the Republican party's fortunes. Consequently, those who approved of the pardon should be more likely than those who disapproved to move toward the Republican Party.

It is also reasonable to argue that one's party identification should be related to one's position along a liberal/conservative continuum. Instead of looking at the performance of the parties, the policies of the parties might be the focus of attention. Since the continuum represents the general policy preferences of the voter, it is preferable to a series of highly specific policy questions about which the voter may have little, if any, concern.[8] Here the respondent has the opportunity to select the issues he or she thinks are important and weight them accordingly. Also, by making use of the simple measure of ideology, we can have some continuity across the panel surveys, with the exception of the 1950s (the item was not asked until the 1970s). If this item serves no other function, it is at least a robust control variable.

Since we are concerned with what influences current party identification, we should take into account past party identification. One option is to use a change score: $PID_t - PID_{t-1}$. If we use a change score, we are, in effect, saying the effect of past party identification on present party identification is 1.00. It is as if we put it on the right-hand side of the equation and constrained the coefficient to be 1.00. Since there is no a priori reason to make this assumption, past party identification is placed on the right-hand side of the equation. Whatever influence past party identification has on current party identification is allowed to show through, rather than being constrained arbitrarily. Placing actual past party identification on the right-hand side of the model is not without problems. The error terms for past and present party identification will undoubtedly be correlated.[9] If this problem is ignored, the estimates of the parameters will be biased and inconsistent. The problem of correlated error terms can be controlled through the use of an instrumental variable.

An instrumental variable for party identification purged of the correlated error component is the result of using several demographic items, such as age, income, gender, race, religion, and the like in an ordered logit equation predicting party identification. This instrument is then used in place of party identification on the right-hand side of the equation predicting current party identification. Unlike some previous works, the instrumental variable in this work does not make use of variables of a more political nature, such as parental party identification, approval of the incumbent administration, or position along a liberal/conservative continuum. Excluding these explicitly political items from consideration when constructing the instrumental variable should minimize the problem of autocorrelation. While the error terms of party identification and political evaluations may well be correlated, the error terms for party identification and the demographic items employed here are not likely to be correlated. The instrumental variable analysis can be found in appendix 3.1 of this chapter. The results are much as one would expect, the R-squareds are low.[10] In spite of this, we can be relatively certain that there is no endogeneity present in the analysis, since it is all but impossible for one's party identification to cause one's race, gender, age, or income. Some might argue that the cure of the instrumental variable is worse than the disease of autocorrelation. Accordingly, I reran the equations below with actual past party identification. These results are presented in appendix 3.2. Fortunately, the major conclusions drawn from the equations are the same regardless of whether actual past party identification or the instrument is used.

Taking all the preceding into account, the model of partisanship to be estimated is:

$$PID_t = f(\text{Retrospective and Prospective economic evaluations,} \\ PID_{t-1}, \text{ and controls})$$

How well does this equation explain the changes in party identification? Table 3.3 presents the equations for the aforementioned model. Given that the dependent variable is not strictly interval, the analysis to follow makes use of ordered logit.[11] As one can see, the equations do a respectable job. The R-squareds, while not tremendous, are quite decent.[12] There is a readily discernable pattern to the size of the R-squareds. It is worth noting that the equations do a better job of explaining changes in party identification in presidential election years. The R-squared for 1960 is greater than that for 1958. The R-squared for 1976 is more than that for 1974. We should note that the presidential election years do have more variables. Two of the presidential election years have the prospective item referencing the respective abilities of the political parties to avoid war. We should also note that there is an upward trend to the R-squareds. Perhaps with the focus on the presidency, people are more inclined to weigh these factors when answering questions concerning their party identification. All the stimulation of the campaign may encourage people to consider their party choices in light of their comparative assessments of the parties. Also, during a presidential campaign there is a national focus that is not present during midterm races. This heightened focus on the presidential candidates of the parties might also encourage citizens to make more of a connection between their evaluations of the parties' relative capabilities and their party identification.

Table 3.3
Party Identification 7-Point Scale as a Function of Retrospective and Prospective Economic Evaluations

	1958	1960	1974	1976	1980W3	1992
RECON	.15/.05	−.04/−.01	−.01/−.00	.22/.09***	−.22/−.16***	.29/.08***
PECON	.63/.27***	.50/.24***	1.49/.36***	.69/.34***	.54/.27***	1.69/.47***
RPOS	.30/.11***	.43/.13***				.14/.04
PWAR		1.20/.35***			.76/.23***	.43/.10***
PARDON			.74/.16***	.81/.16***		
LIB/CON			.29/.16***	.32/.17***	.22/.12***	.38/.19***
PID_{t-1}	1.00/.35***	.89/.27***	.88/.25***	.79/.21*	.80/.21***	.74/.19***
Cut 1	1.23	3.03	2.43	3.25	1.38	4.26
Cut 2	2.31	4.50	3.70	4.86	3.14	5.55
Cut 3	2.67	4.90	4.48	5.64	3.79	6.49
Cut 4	3.02	5.47	5.17	6.35	4.43	7.14
Cut 5	3.36	6.08	5.88	7.36	5.23	8.17
Cut 6	4.49	7.22	7.09	8.84	6.72	9.66
R^2	.08	.16	.13	.17	.15	.21
N	766	749	1060	921	382	754

Note: The first number in each column is the unstandardized ordered logit coefficient. The second number is the standardized coefficient. Asterisk (*) indicates significance at the .10 level, two-tailed; ** indicates significance at the .05 level, two-tailed; *** indicates significanct at the .01 level, two-tailed.

Looking more closely at the individual equations, we can see that our expectations are largely met. All the prospective items are significant at the .01 level, two-tailed with great ease. The retrospective economic items are a mixed bag at best; only in the later years are they statistically significant.[13] In contrast, the retrospective foreign affairs item is significant in the early years, but not in 1992. Not surprisingly, past party identification is statistically significant in each equation.[14]

While noting that the statistical significance of variables is important, it is not the only relevant concern. How important, or powerful, are the variables? Specifically, while the prospective items are statistically significant, are they substantively significant? One way of assessing their importance is to compare their standardized coefficients with those for a variable that is known to be strongly related to party identification—past party identification. Looking at table 3.3, we can see that past party identification, or more accurately its instrument, is only slightly more powerful than the prospective items for the first two panel waves we can see. More interestingly, we can see that the prospective economic items are more powerful than past party identification in the panel waves of 1974, 1976, 1980, and 1992.[15] Similarly, we can see that the non-economic prospective item is more powerful than past party identification in 1960 and 1980. In 1992, the prospective war item is approximately one-half the power of past party identification. Here, the prospective economic item is more than twice as powerful as past party identification.

Aside from comparing these prospective items to past party identification, we should also look at them in relation to the retrospective items. First, we should note that the retrospective economic items are not significant in the panel waves of 1958, 1960, and 1974. In 1976, 1980, and 1992 the retrospective items are statistically significant. Only in 1980 does the retrospective economic item come close to the prospective item in terms of influence on current party identification. In 1980, the retrospective item has roughly 60 percent of the power of the prospective item. In short, the prospective items appear to be important whether we look at them in isolation or in comparison to other variables

Before we delve more deeply into the issue of the relative importance of the retrospective and prospective items, we should look at the 3-point scale of party identification. Brody (1977) has argued that the 7-point scale of party identification is contaminated by short-term forces, but the 3-point scale is not similarly contaminated. It is argued that if we wish to study changes in party identification, we should employ the 3-point scale. The analysis of the 7-point scale has been replicated using the 3-point scale. The results are presented as follows in table 3.4

The analysis of the 3-point scale does nothing to support the argument that it is immune to the forces that influence the 7-point scale of

Table 3.4
Party Identification 3-Point Scale as a Function of Retrospective and Prospective Economic Evaluations

	1958	1960	1974	1976	1980W3	1992
RECON	.19/.06*	-.14/-.04	-.10/-.03	.18/.08**	-.18/-.14**	.21/.06*
PECON	.61/.26***	.55/.27***	1.35/.33***	.58/.30***	.38/.20***	1.62/.46***
RPOS	.33/.11***	.37/.11***				.04/.01
PWAR	1.11/.32***			.82/.25***	.47/.12***	
PARDON			.64/.14***	.75/.16***		
LIB/CON			.25/.15***	.22/.12***	.19/.11**	.31/.16***
PID$_{t-1}$	.99/.37***	.95/.31*	.92/.26***	.93/.27***	.92/.26*	.85/.22***
Cut 1	2.43	4.12	3.23	4.09	2.57	4.83
Cut 2	3.47	5.63	5.31	6.39	4.49	7.24
R^2	.12	.23	.17	.22	.19	.29
N	766	749	1060	921	382	754

Note: The first number in each column is the unstandardized ordered logit coefficient. The second number is the standardized coefficient. Asterisk (*) indicates significance at the .10 level, two-tailed, ** indicates significance at the .05 level, two-tailed, *** indicates significance at the .01 level, two-tailed.

party identification. The pattern of statistical significance in table 3.4 is essentially the same as that of table 3.3. Surprisingly, the only difference of any note at all is that the retrospective economic item is significant for 1958 here, unlike the case with the 7-point scale of party identification. The power of the prospective item compared to party identification is quite strong. The prospective economic item never has less than 70 percent of the power of past party identification. In 1974, 1976, and 1992, the prospective item is stronger than past party identification. The only difference between here and the earlier analysis is that the analysis of the 7-point scale showed that the prospective economic item was also more important than past party identification in 1980. In short, the 3-point scale of party identification seems to be as susceptible to the same political forces as is the 7-point scale.

While these items appear important when looking at statistical significance and when looking at them in comparison to the other variables in the equations, do they have the power to engender much change in party identification? Will movement on these prospective items lead us to predict much movement on the scale of party identification? In short, are the prospective items substantively, as well as statistically, significant? To answer this question, we can make use of the 1958 and 1992 waves of the panel studies. We can compare the probability of scoring as a Republican at varying levels of the other variables. Specifically, if the items other than the prospective economic item are held at the neutral point and the instrument for past party identification is held at the mean, we can see what happens when we vary the score on the prospective economic item.[16] For 1958, if a respondent were to state that the Democratic Party would aid one's finances and that the difference between the parties was major, the analysis suggests that person would have a .07 probability of scoring as a Republican. If, instead of holding a strongly pro-Democratic view, our hypothetical respondent was also neutral on the prospective economic item, the analysis suggests that person would have a .31 probability of scoring as a Republican. Last, if a respondent were to state that the Republican Party would aid one's finances and that the difference between the parties was major, the analysis suggests that person would have a .73 probability of scoring as a Republican. For 1992, taking the individuals in the same order, the probabilities of being a Republican are .05, .22, and .59. One's opinion on the economic future is substantively important. Differences in attitudes on the economic future result in rather dramatic differences in party identification.

There are a few points worth noting at this juncture. First, while party identification does appear to be labile, it is by no means unrelated to previous values. One can see, by looking at the unstandardized and standardized regression coefficients, that past party identification is a strong influence on present party identification. It is clearly an important variable.

Second, it would appear from the equations in tables 3.3 and 3.4, that the retrospective evaluations are of little or no consequence for explaining present party identification. To draw such a conclusion would also be wrong. Downs (1957) suggests that our expectations for the future are wholly determined by our evaluations of the past. People look to the past and extrapolate to the future. The multicollinearity checks performed earlier in this chapter and the previous chapter clearly demonstrate this is not the case. If there were perfect multicollinearity, the equations would not run, as it could not distinguish between the retrospective and prospective items. With near perfect multicollinearity, the equations would have run, but the results would have been nonsensical. This most certainly is not the case. Yet, some relationship between the retrospective and prospective evaluations should be expected. After all, it would be rather surprising if people threw away the information they have concerning the past. If they did throw away this information, it would imply that an incumbent party could get away with anything, as long as it could persuade the electorate that it would do better in the future. We might, however, expect past performance to influence, without determining, our expectations. As Downs (1957) argues, a party that breaks its promises loses credibility. Consequently, a party that has performed badly or contrary to its statements in the past might have difficulty in persuading voters that they will provide a prosperous future and consequently have difficulty in persuading people either to return them to office or, for the purposes of this chapter, to identify with it.

Third, by the construction of the analysis we might have understated the role of past party identification. By looking simply at direct effects equations, we are unable to examine thoroughly the complex paths by which a variable might have an influence on current party identification. Past party identification might influence one's perceptions of the parties relative abilities to provide a prosperous future. Similarly, past party identification might influence the way in which one evaluates the incumbent party's performance. Those of the same party as the incumbent may well give the incumbent party credit for everything good that happened on the incumbent's watch. Conversely, everything bad that happens may well be attributed to forces outside the control of the incumbent party, such as big business, big labor, and other nations.

We should also note that Conover, Feldman, and Knight (1987) have argued that these prospective evaluations are largely a result of partisan rationalizations rather than judgments independent of past partisan affiliation. If the influence of past party identification on these prospective evaluations is powerful, we should have reason to pause. Figure 3.1 below depicts the hypothesis that past party identification has an indirect influence on present party identification. Past party identification works through the retrospective and prospective performance evaluations. From an examination of this model, we should be able to get a better picture of the interconnections among these items.

As we can see in figure 3.1, the analysis is set up so that past party identification can have an influence on these evaluations, but these evaluations cannot have an influence on past party identification. Setting up the model in this fashion does allow past party identification to maximize its influence on current party identification.[17] Also, note that the prospective items can, as depicted in figure 3.1, only have direct effects. In short, the retrospective items and party identification can increase in power because this configuration allows their direct and indirect effects to show, but by design the prospective items cannot increase in power. The results of these analyses are presented in table 3.5. Here, we see that the more complex model shows past party identification to be substantially more powerful than the simple direct effects equation would have led us to believe. Nonetheless, the prospective economic items are a powerful influence on current party identification; never does the prospective economic item have less than 40 percent of the power of past party identification. By looking at the indirect paths, we can also see that the retrospective evaluations are more powerful than originally thought. Regardless, with the single exception of 1980, the prospective economic items are still more powerful than their retrospective counterparts.

Figure 3.1
A Causal Model of Party Identification

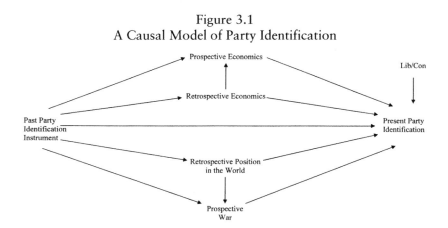

Table 3.5
Direct and Indirect Effects for the 3-Point Scale of Party Identification

	1958			1960			1974		
	DE	IE	TE	DE	IE	TE	DE	IE	TE
PID	.37	.11	.48	.31	.32	.63	.26	.15	.41
RECON	.06	.00[a]	.06	.00[a]	.06	.06	.00[a]	.06	.06
PECON	.26	.00[b]	.26	.27	.00[b]	.27	.33	.00[b]	.33
RPOS	.11	.00[a]	.11	.11	.07	.18			
PWAR				.32	.00[b]	.32			

	1976			1980W3			1992		
	DE	IE	TE	DE	IE	TE	DE	IE	TE
PID	.27	.17	.44	.26	.24	.50	.22	.29	.51
RECON	.08	.10	.18	-.14	-.08	-.22	.06	.06	.12
PECON	.30	.00[b]	.30	.20	.00[b]	.20	.46	.00[b]	.46
RPOS							.00[a]	.03	.03
PWAR				.25	.00[b]	.25	.12	.00[b]	.12

a. The path is insignificant, so it is set to 0.

b. By definition, the indirect paths of the prospective items are 0.

The other concern we had was to what extent these retrospective and prospective economic evaluations are determined by past party identification. We should note that the relationship between past party identification and the retrospective and prospective economic items is typically significant. We should also note that the relationship is by no means determinative. In no year does the R-squared of the ordered logit equation with the prospective economic item as the dependent variable and the retrospective economic item and past party identification as independent variables exceed .15.[18] In short, party identification does not seem to be determining these prospections. It appears that instead of being partisan rationalizations, these prospections may just be that—prospections. Does past party identification determine current retrospective economic evaluations? Here the evidence is even more compellingly negative. The R-squares of these equations are never larger than .03.[19] It would seem quite evident that the retrospective and prospective evaluations, while not completely independent of past party identification, are something more than simply reflections of past party identification.

All that we have seen thus far leads us to the conclusion that party identification is changeable. More important, the changes in party identification that do take place are explicable. People are responding to the political world around them. The findings also support the argument that party identification is not the unmoved mover. We should not automatically assume that party identification influences our evaluations of the political world but is in turn unaffected by the political world. It would appear that the causal arrow points in both directions. Models of vote choice, for example, that include party identification may understate the influence of the other variables in the equation. Models of vote choice that exclude party identification may overstate the influence of these items, as they do appear to be influenced by past party identification. Unfortunately, there is no easy resolution to this matter, as will be evident in subsequent chapters.

For the reader who is not persuaded by the arguments in this chapter, take comfort that the vote choice models to follow do not depend upon your acceptance of the findings in this chapter. Each of the vote choice equations to follow includes party identification. The findings in the subsequent chapters do not hinge on the acceptance of what is here in this chapter. For the reader who accepts the argument presented here in this chapter, take heart. The analysis of vote choice in the chapters to follow would look even stronger without the inclusion of party identification. In sum, regardless of whether the reader accepts the argument I make concerning the changeability of party identification, there is something to be gained through an examination of the remainder of the book.

Appendix 3.1
Instrumental Variables for PID_{t-1}

3-Point Scale

	1956	1958	1972	1974	1980W1	1990
Income	.01	.00	.03***	.05***	.03***	.03**
Labor Union	-.60***	-.57***	-.49***	-.47***	-.66***	-.66***
Urban	-.41**	.07	.01	.00	.01	-.38***
South	-1.70***	-1.41***	-.61***	-.74***	-.32**	-.27**
Age	.01	.02***	.00*	.01***	-.01	-.01***
Black	-.33	-.52	-1.17***	-1.29***	-1.51***	-1.14***
Catholic	-.79***	-1.01***	-.79***	-.89***	-.69***	-.46***
Jewish	-1.19***	-1.17***	-1.30***	-1.56***	-1.11***	-1.37***
Sex	-.13	-.05	.08	.05	.21	.11
Education	.04	.13***	.12***	.11***	.05	.10***
Cut 1	-.48	.01	-.08	.22	-.55	-.69
Cut 2	.67	.95	1.57	2.03	1.10	.87
R^2	.07	.08	.05	.06	.06	.06
N	1092	938	2526	1880	688	1526

(continued)

Appendix 3.1
(*continued*)

7-Point Scale

	1956	1958	1972	1974	1980W1	1990
Income	.01	.01	.03***	.05***	.04***	.04***
Labor Union	-.55***	-.58***	-.52***	-.51***	-.62*	-.72***
Urban	-.32*	.06	.01	-.01	-.03	-.37***
South	-1.48***	-1.36***	-.52***	-.57***	-.27*	-.29**
Age	.00	.01***	.00	.01***	-.01*	-.01***
Black	-.35	-.30	-1.26***	-1.29***	-1.38**	-1.13***
Catholic	-.83***	-.93***	-.78***	-.85***	-.54***	-.47***
Jewish	-1.24***	-1.43***	-1.49***	-1.54***	-1.11***	-1.23***
Sex	-.15	-.13	.03	.04	.19	.11
Education	.04	.09***	.13*	.11***	.04	.08***
Cut 1	-1.72	-1.09	-1.66	-1.01	-1.85	-1.66
Cut 2	-.51	.06	-.16	.17	-.52	-.63
Cut 3	-.20	.35	.33	.79	-.04	-.12
Cut 4	.21	.71	.92	1.45	.57	.33
Cut 5	.64	1.00	1.49	1.98	1.14	.95
Cut 6	1.60	2.14	2.51	3.11	2.54	2.08
R^2	.04	.04	.03	.04	.04	.04
N	1092	938	2526	1880	688	1526

Appendix 3.2
Party Identification as a Function of Retrospective and Prospective Economic Evaluations with Actual Past Party Identification

3-Point Scale

	1958	1960	1974	1976	1980W3	1992
RECON	.26/.05*	.08/.01	-.15/-.03	.12/.04	-.11/-.05	.16/.03
PECON	.32/.09***	.38/.13***	.95/.18***	.50/.19***	.25/.08*	1.20/.27***
RPOS	-.14/-.03	.05/.01				.05/.01
PWAR	.73/.15***		.31/.06	.47/.09***		
PARDON			.32/.05**	.44/.07***		
LIB/CON			.15/.07***	-.01/-.00	.04/.02	.22/.09***
PID$_{t-1}$	3.17/.81***	2.84/.71***	2.40/.65***	2.83/.68***	3.35/.76	2.22/.55***
Cut 1	3.64	4.63	5.65	6.49	6.44	5.07
Cut 2	5.89	7.47	8.78	10.10	9.97	8.52
R^2	.48	.50	.37	.44	.51	.43
N	823	1040	1076	965	426	925

(continued)

Appendix 3.2
(continued)

7-Point Scale

	1958	1960	1974	1976	1980W3	1992
RECON	.16/.03	.07/.01	−.07/−.01	.12/.03*	−.14/−.06**	.27/.08**
PECON	.33/.08***	.32/.10***	1.03/.17***	.49/.17***	.29/.08**	1.14/.24***
RPOS	−.14/−.02	.15/.03*				.12/.03
PWAR	.73/.14***			.30/.05*	.41/.08***	
PARDON			.29/.04**	.38/.05**		
LIB/CON			.14/.05***	.11/.04**	.04/.01	.27/.11***
PID$_{t-1}$	1.37/.84***	1.25/.74***	1.18/.71***	1.32/.72***	1.68/.80***	1.02/.59***
Cut 1	2.15	2.99	2.53	2.59	1.43	4.36
Cut 2	4.24	5.26	4.28	4.81	4.36	6.02
Cut 3	5.17	6.06	5.62	6.19	5.76	7.59
Cut 4	6.14	7.34	6.91	7.43	7.15	8.66
Cut 5	7.02	8.56	8.13	9.20	8.91	10.05
Cut 6	9.04	10.51	9.91	11.33	11.38	12.02
R^2	.08	.36	.29	.34	.40	.33
N	766	1040	1076	965	426	925

Note: The first number in each column is the unstandardized ordered logit coefficient. The second number is the standardized coefficient. Asterisk (*) indicates significance at the .10 level, two-tailed, ** indicates significance at the .05 level, two-tailed, *** indicates significance at the .01 level, two-tailed.

Appendix 3.3
Party Identification as a Function
of Changes in Evaluations

Up to this point, we have considered current party identification as a function of past party identification and the current values of several independent variables. One might argue that the picture is a bit more complex. We are, after all, making an argument about the changeability of party identification. We, perhaps, should look at changes. There are several ways one can do this, and they are presented in the following material. First, we can look at current party identification as being a function of past party identification and the changes in the independent variables. Unfortunately, the only data (using all the variables in the equation) for which this is possible is the 1990–1992 panel study. Second, we make the test even more demanding. We can make the dependent variable the change in party identification and the independent variable the change scores yet again.

The following equations set up the model just as described herein. Specifically, the first column has current party identification as the dependent variable and the independent variables are the instrument for past party identification and the change scores (1992–1990) for the other independent variables. The second column is much like the first with the exception being that instead of the instrument for past party identification, the actual score is in its place. Last, the third column has everything expressed as change scores—including the dependent variable. Consequently, there is no measure of past party identification on the right-hand side of the equation.

How does everything look? Under this more demanding examination, we can see that the prospective economic items shine through rather powerfully. Looking at the first column, we can see that the prospective economic items are almost one-half as powerful as past party identification. Moreover, they are no less than one and one-half times the power of the retrospective economic item. When placed in the even more demanding situation of facing actual past party identification, the prospective economic item does not wilt under the pressure. Here, it has approximately 10 percent of the power of past party identification. Just as before, the prospective economic item is substantially more powerful than its retrospective counterpart. Last, looking at the third column tells us much the same thing. Here, the R-square is substantially lower than the first two equations. This is, no doubt, the result of making the dependent variable a change score. Regardless, the prospective economic item shows through as statistically significant.

Even when we employ the most demanding tests, we can see that changes in party identification are explicable. Before we quickly consign party identification to the position of unmoved (or rarely moved mover), we ought to consider seriously the idea that it is the result of political evaluations. There is an explicitly political component to its makeup.

3-Point Scale

	I	II	III
Party Identification$_{t-1}$	1.27/.40***	2.67/.74***	
Retrospective Economy	.27/.10***	.25/.07*	.10/.05
Prospective Economy	.49/.18***	.58/.15***	.47/.19***
Retrospective World Position	.10/.04	.05/.02	−.03/−.01
Prospective War	.31/.10***	.25/.06**	.17/.06
Ideology	.03/.02	.11/.04	.11/.07
Cut 1	−0.94	0.97	−5.20
Cut 2	0.72	3.96	−2.20
Cut 3			1.73
Cut 4			4.08
R^2	.12	.38	.02
N	615	741	741

Note: The first number in each column is the unstandardized ordered logit coefficient. The second number is the standardized coefficient. * significant at the .10 level, two-tailed, ** significant at the .05 level, two-tailed, *** significant at the .01 level, two-tailed.

I. Instrumental variable for past party identification and change (1992–1990) values for independent variables.
II. Actual past party identification and change (1992-1990) values for independent variables.
III. Party identification and independent variables expressed as change values (1992–1990).

7-Point Scale

	I	II	III
Party Identification$_{t-1}$	1.22/.40***	1.26/.80***	
Retrospective Economy	.28/.11***	.33/.08***	.25/.11***
Prospective Economy	.50/.18***	.60/.14***	.60/.24***
Retrospective World Position	.14/.06	.10/.03	.08/.04
Prospective War	.29/.10***	.21/.04***	.10/.03
Ideology	.05/.02	.12/.04**	.13/.08**
Cut 1	−1.84	0.15	−6.94
Cut 2	−0.87	1.73	−5.84
Cut 3	−0.22	3.29	−4.98
Cut 4	0.13	4.13	−3.80
Cut 5	0.83	5.37	−2.80
Cut 6	1.94	7.16	−1.50
Cut 7			1.08
Cut 8			2.27
Cut 9			3.02
Cut 10			3.73
Cut 11			4.39
Cut 12			5.93
R^2	.07	.30	.03
N	615	741	741

Note: The first number in each column is the unstandardized ordered logit coefficient. The second number is the standardized coefficient. Asterisk (*) indicates significance at the .10 level, two-tailed, ** indicates significance at the .05 level, two-tailed. *** indicates significance at the .01 level, two-tailed.

I. Instrumental variable for past party identification and change (1992–1990) values for independent variables.
II. Actual past party identification and change (1992–1990) values for independent variables.
III. Party identification and independent variables expressed as change values (1992-1990).

Chapter 4

Presidential Elections
A More Comprehensive View

To this point, this work has not directly considered, in a multivariate setting, non-economic influences on voting behavior. Certainly, the earlier chapters have alluded to other explanations of voting behavior, but these other explanations have not been considered alongside the economic evaluations. The previous chapter, for example, is devoted to a single variable, party identification, that is invariably included in models of vote choice. Simply put, we are all aware that there are influences other than economics on voting behavior. By taking these non-economic influences into account, we have a point of comparison. While we should not get into a horse race comparison, it is important to assess the relative importance of these items, so that we can ascertain if the economic items are substantively important. For example, do the economic items have anywhere near the power of party identification? How do they compare to the other influences on voting behavior? If these economic items cross the threshold of statistical significance, are they consequential? If they are statistically significant but substantively unimportant, we have learned little about voting behavior except that we can find yet another statistically significant variable. More important to us is whether these items are substantively consequential. Only by controlling for these other variables that might influence voting behavior will we have any confidence that the economic items have an independent influence on voting behavior. If there is, as one would expect, an intercorrelation among the independent variables, a simple, perhaps simplistic, economic model might overstate the importance of the economic evaluations on voting behavior. An equation that controls for a variety of factors will allow us the opportunity to assess the verisimilitude of the prospective model.

In order to assess the accuracy of the prospective economic model of voting behavior, we should consider several non-economic variables, as well as the economic items. First and foremost, the comprehensive model includes party identification. As the previous chapter stated, no model of voting behavior can be considered complete without party identification. Or, perhaps, the statement should be worded that few will accept a model of voting behavior as complete without the inclusion of party identification.[1] By including party identification, however, the reader should keep in mind that, if the work in the previous chapter accurately describes party identification, the model is stacked against the economic items. If the prospective economic items show through in the face of party identification, not to mention the other independent variables, we can have a great deal of confidence that the prospective economic items have a genuine effect—that there is more than a simple correlation between these prospective economic items and vote choice. Later, to make the argument more complete, a causal model of voting behavior will show party identification to be at the beginning of the process, similar to the funnel of causality argument presented in *The American Voter* (Campbell et al. 1960). If anything, this causal model will be even more stacked against finding the economic items to be of substantive importance than the simple direct effects equation. So again, for the reader who thinks that party identification is the driving force of vote choice, I have set up the equations in such a manner to make it most difficult for the other items to have any influence on voting behavior.

While including party identification is an important step toward putting the economic model of voting behavior through its paces, it is not the only additional variable that we should include. We should also keep in mind that voters might consider non-economic items important when they walk into the voting booth. Fortunately, we can examine the time orientation of the electorate in a non-economic arena. Specifically, there have been many years in which the ANES has had questions concerning foreign affairs. Has the position of the United States in the world improved or deteriorated? What has happened to the prospects for war in the past few years? In 1980, for example, how did voters view Jimmy Carter's handling of the hostage crisis in Iran? All of these items ask the voter to look to the past. We have the opportunity to assess if the voters have rejected or ratified the incumbent administration regarding its past performance in the realm of foreign affairs. Fortunately, the ANES also asks respondents, with some regularity, to state which party, if either, will be better at avoiding war in the upcoming years. In 1996, the voters are asked which party, if either, will be better able to manage foreign affairs. Both of these items are oriented toward the future. As with economic evaluations, the non-economic performance evaluations have a time dimension. By making use of these non-economic items, we have the opportunity to test the hypothesis that voters are looking to the future. If the findings are consistent both across time and across types of policy, we will have greater confidence than if we examine only one time point or one type of policy area.

Aside from these performance items, there is one other item that we should consider. Specifically, we should consider the role that ideology plays in vote choice. Unfortunately, the ANES did not include a measure of ideology until 1972. Of course, we are all aware that a large segment of the voting public does not have a well-defined sense of ideology. Nonetheless, a large percentage of survey respondents, especially when we look at the subset of voters, respond to the question of ideology. Specifically, the survey asks the respondents to place themselves on a 7-point scale of ideology ranging from extremely liberal to extremely conservative. Perhaps, when asked this general question, voters can give a reasoned response that they are unable to offer when asked about specific issues.[2] Because the ideology item loads on the same factor as items they identify as prospective, Miller and Wattenberg (1985) argue that the ideology item is actually prospective. For the purposes of this work, the exact meaning of the ideology item is not terribly consequential. More important is that it be included as a control variable. The last variable to be included in an equation concerns the effect of Watergate on the Republican Party's fortunes. In 1976, voters are asked whether they approve of Gerald Ford's pardon of Richard Nixon. Presumably, those who approve of this particular action will be more inclined to vote for Ford than would those who disapproved of the pardon.[3]

As the reader can easily see in table 4.1, there are a fair number of independent variables in each of the equations for each year. While one would not call this a kitchen sink model, there are a reasonable number of independent variables in each of the equations. Only 1968, with just the two economic items and party identification, seems at all sparse. By examining the entire array of equations, we should be able to draw some reasonable conclusions about what influences voting behavior.

Before we turn to an examination of the individual variables in the equations, we should first assess the explanatory power of these equations. Overall, the equations look good. The pseudo R-squareds are reasonably high. Never do the R-squareds drop below .40, and since 1976 they do not drop below .50. The percentage predicted accurately also gives us reason to think the model performs well. At its worst, the equation predicts 81 percent of the cases accurately—presidential election of 1972.[4] At its best, the equation predicts 91 percent of the cases accurately—presidential election of 2000.[5] In short, a good bit of the variation in vote choice is explained by these equations.

Table 4.1
Presidential Vote Choice: 1956–2000

	1956	1960	1964	1968	1972	1976	1980	1984	1988	1992	1996	2000
RETRO	.05											
RGOV		.02	−.07	−.59*	1.19*	.54*	−.11	.25	.24	.33	−.40	
RPROB												−.05
PROSP	.81*	.86*	.70*	.76*	.97*							
PGOV						1.25*	1.14*					
PPROB								1.64*	1.99*			
PECON										2.14*	.92*	2.03*
RIRAN							−.65*					
RWAR	.51*		−.34*									
RPOS		.08						.49*	.60*	.23	−.75*	−.43
PWAR	1.50*	2.06*	1.74*				.95*	1.48*	1.11*	.94*		.46
FAFFAIRS											1.03*	
L/C					.84*	.47*	.06	.33*	.46*	.78*	.61*	.78*
PARDON						1.06*						
PID	1.53*	1.37*	1.06*	1.98*	1.22*	.83*	1.54*	1.27*	1.21*	1.20*	1.30*	1.70*
CONSTANT	−7.51	−8.12	−5.97	−2.33	−6.88	−9.25	−5.50	−9.53	−10.64	−8.12	−5.44	−8.29
R²	.51	.52	.44	.44	.44	.51	.65	.62	.57	.66	.63	.63
Null	60.8	52.0	67.8	50.7	66.6	52.2	61.0	60.6	55.6	56.2	56.4	50.7
Model	86.7	85.0	84.4	84.1	81.1	85.8	90.6	88.6	87.8	90.3	89.7	89.3
PRE	66.0	71.2	51.5	67.8	43.5	70.4	75.8	71.1	72.5	77.8	76.3	78.3
N	1027	668	789	605	503	833	456	964	852	1018	436	458

Note: Asterisk (*) indicates significance at .05 level, 2-tailed or better. Null percent is the percentage of cases predicted accurately by the equation. PRE is the reduction in error statistic in percentage terms.

An examination of the coefficients in table 4.1 points us to several observations. First and foremost, the prospective economic items are significant in every year, regardless of how economic expectations are measured, regardless of whether the focus is on the individual family or the nation as a whole. Second, the retrospective economic items, while in the expected direction every single time, are surprisingly weak. The retrospective economic items are statistically significant in only three election years: 1968, 1972, and 1976.[6] When we look at the non-economic retrospective and prospective items, the patterns are not quite the same. To be certain, excepting in the 2000 election, the prospective items concerning foreign affairs are significant. The difference comes into play with the non-economic retrospective items. In stark contrast to the economic items, these items are significant in all but three opportunities. For some reason, voters are apparently willing to disregard the past when it comes to economics, but when it comes to foreign affairs they are a less forgiving (or more rewarding) lot. Perhaps voters find it easier to assess the government's responsibility for foreign affairs. Voters may view the position of the United States in the world as being much more clearly within the control of the incumbent administration, so consequently perceptions of changes in the relative position of the United States weighs more heavily in their evaluations of the incumbent administration than do evaluations of past economic performance.

Substantively, do these economic items have the ability to engender much of a change in voting behavior? First, to address that question we can look at what happens to the probability one will support a presidential candidate if the prospective economic evaluations are manipulated. Unlike the earlier, more exploratory chapter, we can consider all the elections. In part, this is so that we can see that one year alone does not drive the model. Table 4.2 shows what happens when we vary the prospective economic evaluations. Briefly, the left most column shows the probability of voting Republican if one is neutral on everything in the equation, except for being of the opinion that the Democratic Party is better able to provide a prosperous economic future. The center column shows the probability of voting Republican if one is completely neutral on everything in the equation. Last, the right most column shows the probability of voting Republican if one is neutral on everything in the equation, except for being of the opinion that the Republican party is better able to provide a prosperous economic future. Given that vote choice is scored 0 = Democratic and 1 = Republican, the probabilities are expressed in terms of voting Republican. If one wants to view it from the perspective of the probability of voting Democratic, one should simply subtract the number present in table 4.2 from 1.00.

Table 4.2
Translation of Table 4.1 into Probabilities of Voting Republican
While Varying the Prospective Economic Variables

	Pro-Democratic	Neutral	Pro-Republican
1956	.14	.64	.95
1960	.08	.54	.94
1964	.10	.46	.88
1968	.18	.68	.95
1972	.45	.76	.90
1976	.10	.66	.96
1980	.10	.52	.91
1984	.28	.67	.91
1988	.13	.52	.89
1992	.13	.28	.77
1996	.12	.25	.45
2000	.09	.44	.86

As one can see, the prospective items have the ability to alter vote choice probabilities considerably. Moving from one extreme to the other changes the probabilities by .72 on average. The minimum change induced is in 1996 with movement of .33 in the probability of voting for a candidate with movement from one extreme to the other on the prospective side. At the other end, movement from believing strongly one party is better able to provide prosperity than the other to the other party being able to provide prosperity induces a change in the probabilities of .86. Before we move on to the regular patterns that are present, it is interesting to note a couple of years as oddities. First, in 1972, those who thought the Democratic Party was better able to provide economic prosperity and were neutral on everything else had a .45 probability of supporting Richard Nixon, the Republican candidate for the presidency. Even more odd, in 1996, those who thought the Republican Party was better able to provide economic prosperity and were neutral on everything else had a .45 probability of supporting Bob Dole, the Republican nominee. To put it bluntly, those who were neutral on everything but the economic item, and on the economic item leaned toward the Republican side, were more likely to vote for the Democratic candidate, Bill

Clinton, than for the Republican candidate, Bob Dole. Still, we should not lose sight of the finding that those who thought the Democrats were better than the Republicans were even more likely to support Clinton.

While there are some oddities present in table 4.2, the information shows that the prospective items have the ability to induce a great deal of change in voting behavior. In every single election, the prospective economic item works as hypothesized. Controlling for everything else, we can see that the prospective economic items have the power to move voters quite a bit. Even in 1996, the weakest year for these items, movement from one extreme to the other induces a change of .33 in the probability of supporting a candidate. Before we move on from this point, we should also note that in all years those who lean toward to the Democratic side on the prospective economic items have a higher probability of voting Democratic than of voting Republican. Furthermore, in all years, except 1996, those who lean toward the Republican Party on the prospective economic item have a higher probability of voting Republican than of voting Democratic.

While looking at the potential for these items to induce changes in voting behavior is important, we should move beyond this examination. To assess more accurately the power of these prospective items, we should make comparisons between them and the other items in the equations. While this should not be taken as a contest among the items, it does provide us a useful vantage point from which to view the relative efficacy of the prospective economic items. Table 4.3 shows the standardized logistic regression coefficients for the equations presented in table 4.1. First, we can look at the power of these prospective economic items compared to the retrospective economic items. Other than 1972, where the retrospective and prospective economic items are virtually equal in power with the retrospective slightly more powerful, the prospective economic items are much more powerful than their retrospective counterparts. Moreover, we should note the relatively few years in which the retrospective economic items cross the line into statistical significance.

A more telling comparison than the one between the retrospective and prospective economic items is the comparison between party identification and the prospective economic items. Here, the prospective items do not fare quite as well. From 1956 through 1972, party identification is substantially more powerful than the prospective economic evaluations. For these years, the prospective economic items have on average approximately 75 percent of the power of party identification. From 1976 through 1992, the prospective economic items are actually more powerful than party identification, averaging 158 percent the power of party identification. Somewhat strangely, we see a return to the numbers

Table 4.3
Presidential Vote Choice: 1956–2000, Standardized Logistic Regression Coefficients

	1956	1960	1964	1968	1972	1976	1980	1984	1988	1992	1996	2000
RETRO	.01	.00	-.02	-.17*								
RGOV					.25*	.17*	-.07	.05	.05	.06	-.10	
RPROB												-.01
PROSP	.29*	.29*	.27*	.31*	.22*							
PGOV						.45*	.36*					
PPROB								.33*	.39*			
PECON										.42*	.21*	.38*
RIRAN							-.26*					
RWAR	.10*		-.08*									
RPOS		.02						.10*	.13*	.05	-.16*	-.08
PWAR	.28*	.42*	.40*				.17*	.29*	.21*	.16*		.08
FAFFAIRS											.23*	
L/C					.36*	.18*	.02	.12*	.18*	.28*	.23*	.78*
PARDON						.15*						
PID	.40*	.34*	.29*	.56*	.33*	.19*	.31*	.27*	.27*	.24*	.30*	.34*

Note: Aseterisk (*) indicates significance at .05 level, 2-tailed or better. This standardization procedure is as discussed in Long (1997).

of the earlier period with the election of 1996. Here, the prospective economic item has 70 percent of the power of party identification. In 2000, the two items have almost the same power. Perhaps over the last thirty or so years the parties have sorted themselves out. Those who were nominally associated with one party have since abandoned their affiliation with their old party for an affiliation with a new party. Perhaps the campaigns of 1996 and 2000 were better than other recent campaigns at activating the partisan predispositions of the electorate. Regardless, party identification has grown in strength.

Aside from the examination of the retrospective/prospective economic items, we should also consider the control variables. One can note that in 1996 the power of ideology relative to the prospective economic item is stronger than it has been in the earlier years. In 1996, the ideology item is modestly stronger than the prospective economic item. In 2000, the ideology item has approximately two-thirds the power of the prospective item. In earlier years, save 1972, ideology was considerably weaker than the prospective economic item. With both ideology and party identification growing in relative strength in 1996, there might be something odd happening in these two presidential election years. We should not forget that the major point is still relevant in this year.

When compared to the retrospective economic items, the prospective economic items show themselves to be a quite strong influence on vote choice. More important, when confronted with party identification, the sine non qua of models of vote choice, the prospective economic items do not wilt. They, instead, show themselves to be a powerful influence on voting behavior.

We might be willing to conclude from the information that has been presented that the prospective economic items are an exceedingly strong influence on voting behavior. Certainly, the information to this point leads us to that conclusion. Given that this is still a somewhat controversial conclusion, we should examine this issue more closely. Although the logistic regression equations do not suffer from excessive multicollinearity, we should put the prospective economic items to an even more stringent and demanding test. Specifically, one can regress, using logistic regression, vote choice on everything (including party identification) in the earlier equations except the prospective economic items. Next, one can then take the residuals from this analysis and regress them, using standard ordinary least squares regression, as they are not a dichotomy, on the prospective economic items. If in the face of this analytic strategy, which assigns all the shared variance between the prospective economic items and the other variables in the equations to the other variables, the prospective items show through as a statistically significant influence on the residuals, we should feel very comfortable in saying that the voters are paying attention to the future when casting a ballot. As the actual equations and their associated coefficients are not readily interpretable, they are not presented.[7] What is important, however, is the direction of the coefficients and the pattern of statistical significance. Here, in spite of assigning all the shared variance between the independent variables and vote choice to the items other than the prospective economic evaluations, the coefficients for the prospective items are both in the expected direction and significantly related at the .01 level (the highest level of significance is .002, two-tailed) to the residuals from the equations that exclude the prospective economic evaluations.[8]

From the results shown in tables 4.1 and 4.3, one might conclude that the prospective items are terribly important and the retrospective evaluations are largely inconsequential. Before we go too far in that direction, we should examine the interrelationships among these independent variables. Specifically, as was argued earlier and shown in the previous chapter, the past, while not wholly determining one's expectations, may well influence one's forecasts. Ignoring that connection would lead us to understate the power and influence of retrospective evaluations on voting behavior. As Becker (1993, 139) stated in his Nobel lecture, "behavior is forward-looking, and it is also assumed to be consistent over time. In particular, individuals try as best they can to anticipate the uncertain consequences of their actions. Forward-looking behavior, however, may still be rooted in the past, for the past can exert a long shadow on attitudes and values."[9] Along these lines, it is important to assess the extent to which the past influences current attitudes and behavior. By making use of path analysis, we can examine the model of voting behavior in a more complex manner that takes into account the interrelationships among the independent variables. As one can see in figure 4.1, the retrospective items are before the corresponding prospective items in the path model. Also, one can see that current party identification is before both the retrospective and prospective items. This is deliberately contrary to the argument made in chapter 3; it biases us toward thinking of party identification as being more important than it might actually be. When we compare the total effects of party identification and the prospective items, the deck is stacked in favor of party identification. For the purposes of assessing the relative importance of the retrospective and prospective items, the alignment of the two types of items in the figure makes both statistical and theoretical sense. Evaluations of the incumbent administration's past performance influence

Figure 4.1
A Causal Model of Presidential Vote Choice

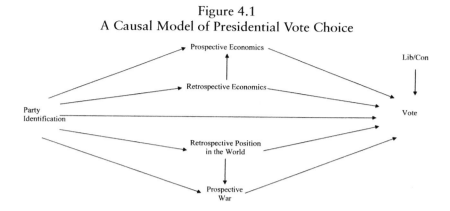

one's evaluations of the parties' relative abilities to provide a prosperous and safe future. Evaluations of the future, however, do not influence one's evaluations of the past.[10]

Many scholars (e.g., Lewis-Beck 1988, 1988b; Markus and Converse 1979; Page and Jones 1979) make use of path models when examining voting behavior. The problem is that when they do this they violate the assumptions by using regression on a dichotomous dependent variable: vote choice, the variable of primary concern. There are at least three strategies that one can employ to get around this problem. First, one can mix analytic techniques. One can use logistic regression for the vote choice portion of the path analytic model and then use ordinary least squares regression for the other portions, as the dependent variables, other than vote choice, are for the most part at least polychotomous. A second strategy is to employ ordinary least squares regression throughout the path analytic section, while recognizing this strategy violates the assumptions of regression. A third strategy, and the one I employ here, is to treat each variable as ordered but not interval when it is a dependent variable. Accordingly, I make use of ordered logit here. I should note that the results from using any one of these techniques leads to similar conclusions.

While it would have been facile to drop the retrospective items from our consideration, as we can see in table 4.4, it would also have been a mistake. We can see that while they do not have terribly strong direct effects, the retrospective economic items are, with only one exception, significantly related to the prospective items. We can also see that the indirect effects of the retrospective economic items are frequently stronger than the direct effects.

Table 4.4
Path Models of Presidential Vote Choice:
Direct, Indirect, and Total Effects

	1956			1960			1964		
	DE	IE	TE	DE	IE	TE	DE	IE	TE
PID	.40	.33	.73	.34	.37	.71	.29	.33	.62
RETRO	.00[a]	.07	.07	.00[a]	.06	.06	.00[a]	−.02	−.02
PROSP	.29	.00[b]	.29	.29	.00	.29	.27	.00	.27
RWORLD	.10	.08	.18	.00[a]	.09	.09	−.08	−.07	−.15
PWAR	.28	.00	.28	.42	.00	.42	.40	.00	.40

	1968			1972			1976		
	DE	IE	TE	DE	IE	TE	DE	IE	TE
PID	.56	.17	.72	.33	.16	.49	.19	.30	.49
RETRO	−.17	.00[a]	−.17	.25	.04	.29	.17	.15	.32
PROSP	.31	.00	.31	.22	.00	.22	.45	.00	.45

	1980			1984			1988		
	DE	IE	TE	DE	IE	TE	DE	IE	TE
PID	.31	.33	.64	.27	.33	.60	.27	.34	.61
RETRO	.00[a]	−.13	−.13	.00[a]	.08	.08	.00[a]	.04	.04
PROSP	.36	.00	.36	.33	.00	.33	.39	.00	.39
RWORLD	−.26	−.04	−.30	.10	.08	.18	.13	.03	.16
PWAR	.17	.00	.17	.29	.00	.29	.21	.00	.21

	1992			1996			2000		
	DE	IE	TE	DE	IE	TE	DE	IE	TE
PID	.24	.33	.57	.30	.28	.58	.34	.22	.56
RETRO	.00[a]	.05	.05	.00[a]	−.04	−.04	.00[a]	−.05	−.05
PROSP	.42	.00	.42	.21	.00	.21	.38	.00	.38
RWORLD	.00[a]	.03	.03	−.16	−.05	−.21	.00[a]	.00[a]	.00[a]
PWAR	.16	.00	.16	.23	.00	.23	.00[a]	.00[a]	.00[a]

a. The path is insignificant, so it is set to 0.

b. By definition the indirect paths of the prospective items are 0.

In fact, one might argue that it is somewhat surprising that the retrospective economic items have any direct effects at all. These effects are limited to just three years: 1968, 1972, and 1976. One might argue that there was something unique about this time that would suggest that voters should be less reliant on their estimations of the future performance of the parties. One thought that comes to mind is the rise in political alienation documented by Arthur H. Miller (1974). Certainly, trust in politicians was dropping to new depths in the late 1960s and early 1970s. We should, however, also keep in mind the prospective model argues that voters should be looking to the future, which they are, but also, that the past should have no direct effect on vote choice. Evaluations of the past, however, do have a demonstrable direct influence on vote choice in three of the presidential election years examined here. Perhaps voters are unwilling to rely entirely on the expectations. They may well temper their expectations by keeping the past in mind when they make the decision as to whom they are going to vote for in the presidential election.

Although one's level of alienation might play a role in whether one relies on retrospections or prospections, we should note that the aggregate pattern does not fit what one would expect if alienation inclined broad segments of the population to rely upon retrospections to a greater extent than they otherwise would. While the retrospective items do attain statistical significance in 1968, 1972, and 1976, aggregate levels of alienation did not decline until the middle of Ronald Reagan's first term (Miller and Borrelli 1991). If aggregate levels of political alienation were the cause of the retrospective items attaining statistical significance, we should observe them as significant throughout the elections since 1968, for even when alienation declined in the mid-1980s, it did not drop that much, nor did it stay low for a terribly long period of time.

We should also look at the non-economic performance items a little more closely than we have to this point. First, as noted earlier, the non-economic retrospective items are significant in every opportunity, save two. More important at this point, however, is how these items fit into the path analysis. As with the economic items, the non-economic items have the same paths. The retrospective items feed into both vote choice (the direct effect) and into the non-economic prospective item (the indirect effect). Here, not surprisingly, the retrospective items are related to the prospective version in every instance.[11] We should also note that these items, like the retrospective economic items, are not a terribly strong influence on the prospective items. The direct effects of the non-economic retrospective items are relatively strong when compared to the indirect effects. That said, however, we should not lose sight of the finding that the non-economic prospective items are typically much stronger than the non-economic retrospective items. Overall, we can see that prospective evaluations have more of an influence on voting behavior than do retrospective evaluations, regardless of whether the evaluation in question is economic or non-economic.

The Swing Voter

One item that we should pay attention to is the swing voter.[12] For those who do not agree with the conclusions drawn in the previous chapter, party identification is the primary factor involved in the voting decision. If this is true, the model is, to some extent, driven by the presence of party identification. Of course, the equations to this point have variables—variables that are central to the thesis of this work—that are significant in the presence of party identification. The remedy from this point of view is not to remove party identification from the equations. That would simply worsen the problem. The shared variation between party identification and these economic items would be now absorbed by items other than party identification. One way, perhaps, of getting around this issue is to truncate the analysis. Instead of looking at the entire data set for each year, we could look exclusively at those who do not have the anchor of party identification pulling them toward a particular vote choice. If we restrict our analysis to just Independents, we are potentially looking at the swing voter, the one who is not swayed by considerations of party. Presumably, independence does not pull one toward a particular party.

Looking more closely at this hypothetical swing voter is useful in that it gives us greater purchase on understanding the dynamics of voting behavior. This segment for whom the pull of party identification is nonexistent is an important portion of the electorate that may ultimately determine who wins the White House. The analysis portion of this section is rather straightforward. We simply repeat the previous analysis with just the Independents. Obviously, since we are just looking at Independents, party identification is not included in the model. After all, it is now a constant.

How does it look when we examine just Independents?[13] Frankly, the picture is not that much different. While the R-squareds are lower, the equations look remarkably similar to those discussed earlier. In terms of significance, the prospective economic items look much like they did before. In 1972, the prospective item is not significant for this subset of voters. Other than that, the prospective items in this subset mirror the significance in the earlier analysis. Overall, the retrospective items look much the same too. Aside from 1984, 1988, and 1996, this subset mirrors the significance in the earlier analysis. In these three years, the retrospective items are statistically significant. In short, it does not appear that the findings from the earlier analysis are being driven by the inclusion of those who identify with a political party.

The Non-Swing Voter

While the swing voter, or Independent, might be the pivot point of the election, particularly in a close election, a more stringent test of the prospective voter might be to look at those with the anchor of party identification to determine if their voting behavior is influenced by these economic considerations. In a sense this would turn the previous analysis on its head. If these economic evaluations have an influence on the voting behavior of the subset of Democratic partisans and the subset of Republican partisans, we should be more confident that these items are of consequence, that the findings are not simply an artifact of looking at the entire sample. Keep in mind that we are looking at models with restricted variation on the dependent variable. Democrats do tend to vote for Democrats and Republicans do tend to vote for Republicans. If these economic items are statistically significant, they have crossed a rather high hurdle.

Having looked at Independents separately, it makes sense to look at Democrats and Republicans separately. Without party identification as a pull on the voting behavior, do these economic evaluations have an influence on how we vote? Briefly, the results show that the same economic factors that work for Independents and for the entire sample also work for each of the partisan subsets.[14] In fact, the same pattern of significance for the entire sample is largely replicated for both Democrats and Republicans. For Democrats the picture is such that there are only two differences. In 1964, the retrospective item is significant, where in the full sample it was insignificant. In 1976, the retrospective item is insignificant, where in the full sample it was significant. Other than these two examples, the economic items work just as they did for the full sample. On the Republican side of the aisle, the picture is similar. In 1968 and 1972, the prospective economic items are not significant. Also, in 1972, the retrospective item is not significant. Last, in 1980, the prospective item drops out of the equation, so we cannot assess the similarity of the equations for the different subsets. In short, we again can see that the prospective items are an influence on voting behavior, no matter how we slice the data.

Conclusion

Looking at the analysis thus far, we can see that the major hypothesis has been consistent with the data. Namely, voters are casting ballots in presidential elections with an eye to the future. We can see that this result is largely consistent for both economic and non-economic considerations. Even when the tests have been set up to make it difficult for the prospective items to show through as important, they do. Now, we need to ask if these findings are limited to presidential elections, the most visible of all elections? Or, are the factors that are important for vote choice in presidential elections relevant for other electoral levels? These are questions for the next chapter.

Chapter 5

Congressional Elections
Yes, the Senate Too

While presidential elections are the mainstay of electoral behavior research, we should investigate other levels of elections. If for no other reason, these other levels of elections provide us additional opportunities to test our theories of electoral behavior. Furthermore, by looking at elections other than at the presidential level, we are able to better understand the subtleties and complexities of electoral behavior. In studies of economic voting, we have found in the past that findings at the presidential level frequently evaporate when the models are tried out at the congressional level (Fiorina 1978; Kinder and Kiewiet 1979, 1981).[1] When we look at multiple levels of elections, we will be able to learn if voters take different considerations into account when casting their ballots at different levels. We will be able to learn if voters look upon people running for office as part of a team, or at least take their global evaluations of the parties' into account when casting their ballots. Or, are candidates in House or Senate races able to separate themselves from their respective parties?[2] Candidates may try to downplay their ties to the national party organization for explicitly electoral reasons. Perhaps they fear that being tied too closely to a figure in the national party will hinder their chances of election, or reelection.[3] Individual members of Congress, for example, frequently try to present themselves as the only one (or perhaps one of the few) that is actually doing a good job. If there are differences between electoral levels, are there readily apparent features of the election type or the electoral period that help to explain the differences? To what extent are candidates able to distance themselves from their respective national party organizations? To these ends, this chapter looks at both House and Senate elections.[4]

Hinckley (1981) argued the study of congressional elections is woefully underrepresented in studies of voting behavior. While this is not as

77

true as when she wrote that statement, it still is the case that compared to presidential elections, congressional elections are under studied. Furthermore, when we look at congressional elections, we can see the Senate is the cast off sibling. By looking at the House and Senate, we can get a better sense of how electoral arrangements and the number of people in a chamber influence the voters.

Should we expect any differences across levels of elections? It is at least reasonable to think that there might be differences. Presidential elections receive a great deal of media coverage. Voters, while not terribly well informed about the presidential candidates, are better informed about the presidential contest than they are about House and Senate elections (Hinckley 1981; Mann 1978; Mann and Wolfinger 1980; and Stokes and Miller 1966). All the attention the media devote to presidential elections may make it likely that voters consider different factors when voting in presidential elections than when voting in House and Senate elections. Because of this relative abundance of information, voters may be able to cast what we consider to be a relatively well-informed vote in presidential elections, at least in comparison to House and Senate elections.

Aside from candidates trying to distance themselves from their national parties, voters also have reasons to divorce their considerations of the national parties from their decision-making process concerning congressional elections. While each chamber of the legislature might be the policymaking equal of the president, no individual member of either chamber comes close to matching the power of the president. Even members that hold leadership positions, such as the Speaker of the House or majority leader of the Senate, do not possess the same policymaking power of the president. Consequently, a voter in a congressional election may have little reason to use the ballot to indicate how the government should be run in the future. Instead of looking at what the entire government does or what a chamber of the legislature does, the voter has an incentive to examine only those things over which the individual member of Congress might reasonably be expected to exert some influence. Consequently, the items that influence voters in congressional races may well be very different than those that influence voters at the presidential level.

Should we expect any differences across levels of congressional elections? Are House and Senate elections different from each other? First, given the respective sizes of the two chambers, we should probably see the economic items as stronger in Senate elections than in House elections. In general, individual members of the Senate have greater opportunities to influence the national policymaking process than do individual members of the House of Representatives. Consequently, voters are more likely to take these national candidate and party evaluations into account in Senate elections than in House elections. Second, with the smaller constituency for most House seats, we might expect personal considerations to matter more in House elections than in Senate elections. Third, Senate contests are much more visible contests than are House contests (Bullock and Scicchitano 1982). The quality of candidates is typically higher in Senate contests than in House contests, especially for challengers (Jacobson 2001). Consequently, we should expect there to be some differences. Every factor pushes us toward the expectation that Senate contests will be influenced by these national considerations to a greater extent than will House races.

Let us not make too much of the differences across electoral levels we might expect to see. There are still some similarities that are likely to be shown. The economic evaluations that were important in explaining presidential elections are likely to be influential in lower level races. Why? If individual members of Congress are not viewed as having a great deal of power over national events, why should voters take these evaluations of the national parties into account when voting in congressional elections? One simple explanation is that voters might try to economize on the collection of information. Once a voter has taken the time to become familiar with the national candidates of a party, or the party in general, that voter might well believe that information is relevant for the lower level contests, as well as the presidential contest. It is reasonable to assume that there is some degree of commonality with regard to policymaking across members of a party. Certainly, there are some people within a party that deviate greatly from the party orthodoxy with a great deal of regularity, but it is not the norm. We have seen repeatedly that Democrats tend to vote with Democrats and Republicans tend to vote with Republicans (Bullock and Brady 1983; Clausen 1973). If voters are loosely aware of the commonality among members of the respective parties, they would be acting quite rationally to reduce the amount of information needed to cast an informed ballot. Instead of looking at the individual congressional candidates and making a decision, voters may instead employ evaluations of the party when casting a ballot in an individual congressional contest.

In addition to the differences across levels of elections, we should also examine the issue of timing. On-year and off-year races may have different dynamics. With a national campaign being waged by presidential candidates, voters may be more likely to consider these party and presidential candidate evaluations in their decisions than they are in off-year races that are typically waged in a period of relative political calm. During presidential election years, the amount of time devoted to political campaigns by the media is greater than it is during off-year races. Additionally, as the media covers the national parties more during on-year races than off-year races, voters are likely to have an easier time getting information about the national parties during this time than during off-year races. In fact, one might argue that potential voters have difficulty avoiding political information during presidential election years.

While evaluations of the national parties and candidates are likely to influence voting behavior in congressional elections, there are likely to be some level-specific factors at work in these congressional elections. If the equations to follow do not take these level-specific factors into account, we may well draw some erroneous conclusions. Perhaps the most studied, some might say over studied, phenomenon in American politics is the incumbency advantage. As Charles O. Jones (1981, 458) stated, "that one more article demonstrating that House incumbents tend to win reelection will induce a spontaneous primal scream among all congressional scholars across the nation." While I have no desire to induce such a scream, Jones's statement does tell us that no model of vote choice in congressional elections can be considered complete without an incumbency variable. While one can simply put in a single variable for incumbency, this would not tell us anything we do not already know; incumbents are more likely to get votes than are challengers or open seat candidates. We should be cognizant of the possibility that incumbency can work for one party but not the other in a particular year.[5] One can imagine, for example, that Republican incumbents might have actually been hurt by their incumbency status in 1974. Being a part of the same party as the president during the White House scandal might have inclined voters to hold those Republicans more culpable than open seat Republican candidates. Instead of actually hurting Republican congressional incumbents, it definitely would not be surprising if the effects of Watergate kept Republican incumbents from being able to exploit the incumbency advantage to its fullest. Democrats, in contrast, might have been able to magnify the effects of incumbency. More likely, one can imagine that even if the incumbency advantage is working for both parties' congressional candidates, it might well have differential strength for the candidates of each party. Instead of simply coding the incumbency variable simply -1 for Democratic incumbents, 1 for Republican incumbents, and 0 for open seats and expecting a positive coefficient for the item (as vote choice is scored 0 = Democratic vote and 1 = Republican vote), the equations to follow have two variables: Republican incumbent, scored 1 if there is a Republican incumbent and scored 0 if the seat is open or is held by a Democrat; Democratic incumbent, scored 1 if there is a Democratic incumbent and scored 0 if the seat is open or is held by a Republican.[6] Here, of course, the expectation is that the Republican incumbent variable will have a positive sign and the Democratic incumbent variable will have a negative sign. By considering incumbency in this manner, we can learn more than incumbents are more likely than challengers and open seat candidates to get votes. We can get a better sense of whether the incumbency advantage plays out differently for the two parties.

Should we expect there to be a partisan component to the incumbency advantage? Looking at some of the literature on divided government points in one direction. Democratic incumbents, according to Jacobson (1990), should be better able than Republican incumbents to make use of the advantages of office. According to Jacobson (1990), people have different expectations for presidents and members of the House. We expect the president to provide economic prosperity and manage the problems of unemployment and inflation. In short, we expect the president to pursue broad national interests. We expect members of Congress, however, to look out for the interests of the district. These institutional expectations, according to Jacobson, overlap with our partisan expectations. Democrats, according to Jacobson, are better at looking out for the interests of the poor and the middle class and at handling problems such as unemployment. In short, according to Jacobson, Republicans provide economic efficiency while Democrats ameliorate the problems of those who suffer under an efficient economic system. Accordingly, the citizenry typically favors Republican presidential candidates and Democratic House candidates.

If congressional careers are built upon the edifice of new programs and delivering particularized benefits to constituents, congressional Democrats should benefit. Republicans, in contrast, that have a more minimalist conception of government, those who view government as part of the problem, not the solution, should be less attracted to government service. Even when they do win office, Republicans, according to this formulation, should grow disenchanted with holding government office and not be as inclined as Democrats to participate in the provision of particularized government benefits to their constituents. Given that Republicans, according to Jacobson, are less inclined to use the levers of government to provide particularized benefits for their constituents, we should not be surprised to see that Republicans are less likely to have long-lived congressional careers. Instead, we should see that Republicans are more likely to leave Congress voluntarily than are Democrats. Jacobson (1990) points out that that is just what we observe in the 1980s. Because these partisan and institutional expectations overlap, there should be a disproportionate advantage for Democratic House incumbents.[7] If Jacobson is right, the magnitude of the incumbency advantage and Democratic advantage should be larger in the House of Representatives than in the Senate, as members of the House are likely to be more focused on specific particular district needs, as they typically have smaller districts than do members of the Senate. Members of the House, as argued earlier, are also likely to be judged more on the provision of particularized benefits to individuals and to the district than are members of the Senate.

While Jacobson's (1990) discussion of divided government leads us to predict a disproportionate Democratic incumbency advantage, Fiorina's (1996) policy balancing explanation of divided government is not so explicit. One can, however, make some reasonable inferences from the policy balancing model as it relates to a partisan bias to the incumbency advantage. According to Fiorina, voters select divided government to balance the extremes of both parties. If voters, in part, select divided government to keep any one party from controlling the entire government, there should not be a partisan bias to the incumbency advantage. Incumbents of both parties should be equally able to take advantage of the perquisites of office and use them to gain an advantage over their challengers when seeking reelection. There is, however, a potentially confounding factor. If voters are using the Congress to balance the executive branch, there should be a bias toward the Democratic Party when the Republicans control the White House, especially during the midterm races when continued Republican control of the White House is assured. In on-year races, the bias toward the Democratic Party should, in part, be a function of whether voters think the Republicans will win the White House. This bias, if it exists, however, should apply across the board, not just to incumbents. For this reason, we would expect there to be no difference between Republican and Democratic incumbents in terms of the incumbency advantage. The partisan bias of any particular year should be reflected in the intercept, not in the coefficients for the two incumbency variables.[8]

The House

As the model is set up, we can now see whether legislative elections conform to expectations. Table 5.1a shows us the logistic regression equations for vote choice in the House elections of 1956 through 2002. What is most striking is the similarity to the equations for vote choice in presidential elections. The retrospective economic items are not significant all that often. In only five years do they cross the .05 two-tailed threshold of statistical significance. Given that we have data for almost twice as many House election years as we do for presidential election years, this is not a terribly dissimilar result from chapter 4 where we saw that the retrospective items were significant three times. The prospective items are significant in most of the elections. In only the elections of 1960, 1978, and 1998 are the prospective items not significant at the .05 level, two-tailed.[9] The factors that influence voters in House elections seem to be similar to those that influence voters in presidential elections.

Table 5.1a
House Vote Choice: 1956–2002

	1956	1958	1960	1964	1968	1972	1974	1976	1978	1980	1982
RETRO	.28	.45*	.12	.05	-.13						
RGOV						-.06	.50*	.14	-.13	.14	.52*
PROSP	.35*	.49*	.23	.51*	.32*						
PGOV						.63*	.96*	.30*	.19	.43*	.73*
PPROB											
PECON											
RIRAN										-.17	
RWAR	.32			-.15							
RPOS		.15	.00								
PWAR	.70*		1.17*	.66*						.36	
L/C						.17	.08	.23*	.33*	.25*	.25*
PARDON							.78*	.42			
PID	1.72*	2.03*	1.50*	1.13*	1.42*	1.18*	1.13*	1.09*	1.43*	.81*	1.37*
HDEM	.88	-.31	-.25	1.10*	-.79*	-.74*	-1.34*	-1.46*	-1.83*	-1.41*	-.71
HREP	2.60	.88*	.74	2.00*	.27	.98*	.33	.84*	1.44*	.90	1.27*
CONSTANT	-8.39	-5.05	-5.06	-5.44	-1.61	-2.99	-4.29	-3.22	-2.49	-3.87	-6.41
R^2	.50	.47	.42	.33	.27	.31	.33	.35	.43	.33	.49
Null Percent	73.9	53.9	53.9	65.2	51.6	54.1	59.6	54.2	51.5	50.1	53.9
Model Percent	86.8	86.1	83.7	80.4	77.3	77.2	78.3	78.0	82.3	77.9	86.7
PRE	49.4	69.8	64.6	43.7	53.1	50.3	46.3	52.0	63.5	55.6	69.8
N	629	584	577	655	568	434	562	646	633	416	421

(continued)

Table 5.1a
(continued)

	1984	1986	1988	1990	1992	1994	1996	1998	2000	2002
RETRO										
RGOV	−.00	.25	.42*	.15	.06	−.14	−.01			.18
RPROB								−.04	−.46*	
PROSP										
PGOV										
PPROB	.90*	.77*	.70*						.56*	
PECON				1.13*	.69*	.61*	.56*	.37		1.13*
RIRAN										
RWAR		−.14								
RPOS	.09		−.15	−.11	.01	−.20	−.12	−.03	−.42	.12
PWAR	.41*	.45*	.43*	.17	.55*				.43	
FAFFAIRS							.55*	.33		
L/C	.24*	.37*	.39*	.28*	.25*	.44*	.24*	.55	.36*	.31*
PID	.63*	.95*	.91*	.98*	.76*	1.22*	1.22*	1.19*	1.17	.93*
HDEM	−1.99*	−1.14*	−1.78*	−1.70*	−.88*	−1.40*	−.51	−.97*	−1.27*	−1.80*
HREP	.87*	1.56*	1.52*	1.15*	1.16*	.88*	1.52*	1.53*	1.30*	.11
CONSTANT	−3.46	−4.79	−5.46	−4.70	−3.18	−2.62	−4.42	−4.76	−2.88	−4.13
R²	.40	.41	.45	.44	.34	.42	.45	.43	.47	.45
Null Percent	50.8	51.6	54.6	59.2	57.5	54.5	54.3	50.7	50.4	57.5
Model Percent	78.6	81.5	83.0	82.1	79.4	81.0	83.1	80.7	83.6	81.7
PRE	56.5	61.8	62.6	56.1	51.5	58.2	63.0	60.9	66.9	56.9
N	791	281	605	458	1007	732	427	363	389	534

Note: Asterisk (*) indicates significance at .05 level, 2-tailed or better.

While the factors that influence voting behavior are similar across the levels of election, we should also examine if these prospective items have the power to induce much change in voting behavior. Does movement from one extreme to the other engender much change in the probability that one's voting behavior will change? To this end, we can examine table 5.1b to ascertain what can happen to an individual's voting behavior when we put all the other variables at neutral and vary the prospective economic items. We can

Table 5.1b
Translation of Table 5.1a into Probabilities of Voting Republican
While Varying the Prospective Economic Variables

	Pro-Democratic	Neutral	Pro-Republican
1956	.02	.05	.13
1958	.14	.42	.76
1960	.28	.43	.60
1964	.04	.16	.47
1968	.39	.63	.81
1972	.31	.46	.62
1974	.36	.60	.79
1976	.48	.63	.76
1978	.45	.54	.63
1980	.40	.61	.79
1982	.15	.42	.76
1984	.45	.67	.83
1986	.28	.46	.65
1988	.30	.46	.63
1990	.24	.49	.75
1992	.29	.44	.61
1994	.43	.58	.72
1996	.26	.38	.51
1998	.26	.34	.42
2000	.27	.40	.53
2002	.39	.66	.86

see that their power varies tremendously from year to year. In the first year (1956) that we examine, we can see that the prospective economic item does not appear to be able to engender that much change. A voter who is pro-Democratic on the prospective economic item and who is neutral on all other items has a .02 probability of voting Republican. If we shift this voter to having pro-Republican sensibilities on the prospective economic item, the probability shifts to .13. While one might try to twist this by saying the probability of voting Republican has increased by 600 percent, that would not be an honest depiction of what is really occurring. The more accurate point is that the probability shifted very little. Also, the probability of a completely neutral person on everything save the prospective economic item voting Republican is very low regardless of the stand the voter takes on the prospective economic item. One election later, however, the differences are much more stark. One who is completely neutral on everything but is pro-Democratic on the prospective economic item has a .14 probability of supporting the Republican House candidate. One who is completely neutral has a .42 probability of supporting the Republican House candidate. In contrast, one who is completely neutral on everything but is pro-Republican on the prospective economic item has a .76 probability of supporting the Republican House candidate. While most years are not quite as stark as 1958, the overwhelming pattern is that these prospective items can make quite a difference in one's voting behavior. In most years, crossing from one end to the other means a change from one party's House candidate to the other party's House candidate, usually by a large margin.

Aside from simply ascertaining whether these items have the ability to induce changes in voting behavior, we should also see how they compare to other items in the equation, such as party identification and incumbency status. As we can see in table 5.1c, compared to party identification, these prospective economic items are strong. They do not always equal or exceed the power of party identification, but the prospective economic items are consistently one-quarter or better the power of party identification. In the more recent years, they have come close to equaling the power of party identification. Indeed, in 1984, the prospective economic item was more powerful than party identification. From 1980 through 1996, the prospective economic items have had at least 40 percent the power of party identification. In 2002, the prospective economic item has approximately the same power of party identification. While the comparison of the prospective items to party identification is rather straightforward, the comparison of the prospective items to incumbency status is a bit more complicated, as there are two incumbency variables (one for each party) in each equation. The most important point we should note is the prospective economic items do not wilt under exposure to the incumbency variables.

Table 5.1c
House Vote Choice: 1956–2002
Standardized Logistic Regression Coefficients

	1956	1958	1960	1964	1968	1972	1974	1976	1978	1980	1982
RETRO	.06	.11*	.03	.01	-.05						
RGOV						-.02	.12*	.06	-.05	.12	.13*
PROSP	.14*	.16*	.09	.23*	.16*	.17*					
PGOV							.21*	.14*	.06	.21*	.29*
PPROB											
PECON											
RIRAN											
RWAR	.07			-.04						-.10	
RPOS		.04	.00								
PWAR	.14*		.30*	.18*						.10	
L/C						.09	.05	.12*	.16*	.14*	.11*
PARDON							.15*	.08			
PID	.48*	.62*	.46*	.36*	.49*	.39*	.35*	.33*	.38*	.25*	.37*
HDEM	.14	-.05	-.04	.22*	-.17*	-.15*	-.26*	-.28*	-.31*	-.27*	-.12
HREP	.42	.15*	.12	.38*	.06	.18*	.06	.15*	.24*	.17	.20*

(continued)

Table 5.1c
(continued)

	1984	1986	1988	1990	1992	1994	1996	1998	2000	2002
RETRO										
RGOV	-.00	.06	.11*	.04	.01	-.04	-.00			.07
RPROB								-.01	-.10*	
PROSP										
PGOV										
PPROB	.25*	.18*	.16*						.14*	
PECON				.27*	.21*	.15*	.16*	.10		.31*
RIRAN										
RWAR		-.03								
RPOS	.03		-.04	-.03	.00	-.05	-.03	-.01	-.10	.03
PWAR	.11*	.10*	.10*	.03	.14*				.09	
FAFFAIRS							.15*	.08		
L/C	.11*	.16*	.18*	.13*	.14*	.21*	.12*	.26*	.17*	.16*
PID	.19*	.28*	.25*	.28*	.24*	.36*	.35*	.33*	.31	.26*
HDEM	-.35*	-.20*	-.29*	-.30*	-.17*	-.25*	-.09	-.16*	-.21*	-.30*
HREP	.14*	.27*	.24*	.19*	.20*	.15*	.26*	.27*	.22*	.02

Note: Asterisk (*) indicates significance at .05 level, 2-tailed or better.

Is there a pattern to these House races that fits the pattern of presidential elections? Do the prospective items appear to have more power in on-year races than in off-year races? Aside from the pattern of these prospective items becoming relatively stronger over time, there does not appear to be any on-year/off-year cycle to their power relative to party identification. If we simply look at the amount of change that is likely to take place from moving from one extreme to the other on the prospective item, we see again that there is not the expected pattern. The average change induced by moving from one extreme to the other in on-year races is approximately .32. In off-year races, the average change is .40. Simply put, the evidence is just the opposite of the argument made previously. It would seem, at least in House elections, voters are moved quite a bit by these prospective items in both on-year and off-year races.

How does incumbency fair in House elections? While fearing the primal scream of my colleagues everywhere, I must say incumbents do well electorally. In general, incumbents are better able to get the votes of the citizenry than are challengers or open seat candidates. Having said that, let me hasten to add that the picture is not quite as simple as we might have thought. First, there are two years for which incumbency is not significant at all. Neither Democratic or Republican incumbents appear to be significantly advantaged in either 1956 or 1960. We should note that both of these years are prior to the often written about increase in the incumbency advantage. What is more interesting is the number of times that incumbency fails to achieve statistical significance after the rise in the incumbency advantage. In six opportunities from 1968 forward one of the incumbency variables fails to achieve statistical significance at the .05 level (Republican: 1968, 1974, 1980, and 2002; Democratic: 1982 and 1996). Looking at these post-rise in the incumbency advantage years, one sees very little in the way of a pattern. Yes, the Republicans do poorly in 1974 (a bad year for Republicans), but they also do poorly in 1980 (a good year for Republicans). We see the same lack of a pattern for Democrats. One of the years for which the Democratic incumbency variable is not significant is a good year (1982) another is, at best, a fair year (1996). Looking at these incumbency variables in conjunction with the constant, however, helps to illuminate the matter. In 1968 and 1980, the constant shows that there was less of a Democratic slant to the electorate than in most other years. The constant for 1974 is virtually the same as the average constant for all the years. In short, the Republicans simply had a terrible year in 1974. Looking at the other side of the ledger, we see that the two years in which the Democratic incumbency variables were not significant were also years when there was a greater than average Democratic slant to the electorate, with 1982 being more decidedly so. It appears that in four of the five years (obvious exception: 1974) in which incumbency was not terribly beneficial to a party's candidates, there was a strong slant in the electorate toward that party.

How do the incumbency variables look over time? Are Republican or Democratic House incumbents more advantaged by incumbency? We can examine the standardized logistic regression coefficients in table 5.1c to answer this question. Simply counting up the number of years in which one party is more advantaged than the other tells us that there is not much of a difference: the Democratic incumbency variable is the more powerful ten times and the Republican incumbency variable is the more powerful eleven times. Looking at the ratio of the standardized logistic regression for Democratic incumbency to that for Republican incumbency, we can see that there is a bias toward Democratic incumbents. The ratio is 1.92:1.00 on average. If we exclude 2002 as an atypical year, the ratio drops to 1.27. We should note that the Democratic advantage relative to the Republican advantage is larger in the latter years. Four of the eleven times the Republican advantage exceeds the Democratic advantage are the first four election years of the study.

The Senate

How does the Senate look? The results from the Senate look like the results from the other sections of this book. The retrospective economic items are statistically significant in only four years. The prospective economic items are insignificant in only five years. The Senate equations explain less variation in vote choice than do the House equations, which in turn explain less than the presidential vote choice equations.

Do the prospective items have the ability to influence vote choice dramatically? Looking at table 5.2b, we can see that these evaluations can make quite a difference. In 1956, the first year of the analysis, we see that one who is completely neutral except for believing that the Democratic Party is better able to provide economic prosperity has a .20 probability of supporting the Republican Senatorial candidate. Someone who is completely neutral on everything has a .44 probability of supporting the Republican Senatorial candidate. Finally, a citizen who is completely neutral except for believing that the Republican Party is better able to provide economic prosperity has a .71 probability of supporting the Republican Senatorial candidate. If one looks over the entire table, one sees that typically the differences between the probabilities of voting Republican for those who believe that the Democratic Party will provide prosperity and those who believe that the Republican party will provide economic prosperity are quite strong.

Table 5.2a
Senate Vote Choice: 1956–2002

	1956	1958	1960	1964	1968	1972	1974	1976	1978	1980	1982
RETRO	.22	.29	.15	.23*	-.60*						
RGOV						.04	.19	-.04	.10	-.07	.06
PROSP	.38*	.34*	.56*	.18*	.31*						
PGOV						.35	.81*	.53*	.60*	.27	.95*
PPROB											
PECON											
RIRAN										-.26*	
RWAR	.27			-.21*							
RPOS		.30	.02								
PWAR	.78*		1.14*	.72*						.30	
L/C						.03	.18	.34*	.13	.14	.30*
PARDON							.36	.26			
PID	1.60*	2.18*	1.37*	1.45*	1.43*	1.16*	1.22*	.97*	1.19*	.92*	1.29*
SDEM	-1.07*	-1.92*	-.79	-1.19*	-.18	.43	.00	-.71*	-.47	-.71*	-1.87*
SREP	.25	-.25	.77	-.46*	.79*	1.43*	1.42*	.26	.75*	.51	.27
CONSTANT	-5.51	-4.06	-5.27	-2.70	-.83	-2.54	-4.59	-3.92	-4.51	-2.11	-5.56
R²	.46	.49	.44	.33	.28	.21	.32	.29	.26	.29	.49
Null Percent	51.2	56.3	52.5	60.2	50.1	51.9	56.2	56.3	50.8	50.6	53.5
Model Percent	84.5	85.7	83.6	80.1	78.3	70.5	77.8	76.5	74.7	75.2	82.9
PRE	68.2	67.3	65.5	50.0	56.5	38.7	49.3	46.2	48.6	49.8	63.2
N	729	510	354	537	423	264	441	510	376	334	357

(continued)

Table 5.2a
(*continued*)

	1984	1986	1988	1990	1992	1994	1996	1998	2000	2002
RETRO										
RGOV	.21	.20	.28	.25	.30*	-.34*	.13			.22
RPROB								-.31	-.79*	
PROSP										
PGOV										
PPROB	.66*	1.12*	.73*							
PECON				.58*	.89*	.95*	.37	.18	.47	1.19*
RIRAN										
RWAR		.33								
RPOS	.30*		.02	-.03	.06	-.21	-.39	-.44*	-.10	.19
PWAR	.52*	.19	.33	.19	.31*				-.07	
FAFFAIRS							.49	.90*		
L/C	.02	.23	.36*	.32*	.39*	.55*	.62*	.27*	.61*	.57*
PID	1.04*	1.06*	.92*	1.03*	.68*	.87*	1.37*	1.19*	1.47*	1.21*
SDEM	-.90*	-.00	-.68*	-1.82*	-.73*	-.98*	-.46	-.60	-1.41*	-1.33*
SREP	.71*	.90	1.30*	.04	.34	.34	.59	1.02	.03	.32
CONSTANT	-4.77	-6.18	-5.69	-3.62	-4.06	-2.82	-5.01	-3.16	-2.48	-6.30
R²	.33	.36	.35	.30	.33	.40	.47	.43	.45	.53
Null Percent	50.5	54.2	53.4	55.2	54.0	57.5	50.6	53.2	54.2	52.7
Model Percent	77.9	81.7	77.7	76.0	79.6	81.0	84.2	83.9	82.1	86.2
PRE	55.4	60.0	52.1	46.4	57.4	55.3	68.0	65.6	60.8	70.8
N	497	251	620	337	897	654	259	329	308	347

Note: Asterisk (*) indicates significance at .05 level, 2-tailed or better.

Table 5.2b
Translation of Table 5.2a into Probabilities of Voting Republican
While Varying the Prospective Economic Variables

	Pro-Democratic	Neutral	Pro-Republican
1956	.20	.44	.71
1958	.33	.56	.79
1960	.22	.59	.89
1964	.55	.68	.78
1968	.35	.58	.79
1972	.30	.38	.46
1974	.19	.34	.64
1976	.29	.54	.77
1978	.21	.47	.74
1980	.32	.44	.57
1982	.21	.63	.92
1984	.32	.48	.64
1986	.13	.32	.59
1988	.19	.33	.51
1990	.50	.65	.76
1992	.29	.48	.68
1994	.29	.51	.73
1996	.31	.39	.48
1998	.34	.38	.43
2000	.35	.46	.58
2002	.22	.48	.75

There are, however, what appear to be some oddities. In 1964, for example, a person who is completely neutral except for believing the Democratic Party is better able to provide economic prosperity has a .55 probability of supporting the Republican Senatorial candidate. This may, in part, be explained by the skewed nature of the distribution on the prospective item. Over 90 percent of the respondents had either a neutral or pro-Democratic Party opinion on the prospective item in 1964. Nonetheless, the overall pattern is quite strong. On average, the difference in the probability of voting Republican between those who believe that the Democratic Party would be better at providing a prosperous future and those who believe that the Republicans would be better at providing a prosperous future is .38. The overall picture is that these items are of import, even after controlling for a wide variety of other influences on vote choice.

How does incumbency work in Senate elections? Most strikingly, we can note that it is not as consistent as it was in the House elections. Incumbency is significant in but thirteen of twenty-one opportunities for Senate Democrats, and in only eight of twenty-one opportunities for Senate Republicans. As we might have anticipated, incumbency is much weaker here than it is in House races. We should note that there is not a pattern to the significance across time. It is not as if the incumbency variables were insignificant early on and then became significant in the more recent years. Instead, it simply seems as though there is random fluctuation across time. One should note, however, there does appear to be a pattern for Republicans. The significant years are in the middle. The incumbency item is insignificant until 1964, and it has not been significant since 1988. With the incumbency variables insignificant in so many years, we should be somewhat cautious in our examination of the relative power of incumbency for the two parties. Incumbency appears to be more important for Senate Democrats than for Senate Republicans, as the incumbency variable is more powerful for the Senate Democrats thirteen of twenty-one opportunities. As this advantage does not hold consistently, nor is the incumbency variable consistently significant for either party, we should not make too much of this finding. We should not be terribly surprised by the relative weakness of incumbency in Senate elections. Part of the incumbency advantage is the result of the actions of the incumbent. Part, however, is also the result of the identity of the challenger. If a member of Congress is facing a weak challenger, we should expect that incumbent to do rather well; the incumbent's advantage should look very strong. If one is, however, facing a strong challenger, the incumbent's advantage will, no doubt, be muted. Given that Senate challengers are typically of higher quality than are House challengers (Jacobson 2001), we should expect incumbency to be more powerful in House elections than in Senate elections.

Table 5.2c shows the standardized logit coefficients for the Senate equations. When we look at the various items in the Senate equations, we can see that the prospective items are consequential. While the prospective economic item only has a standardized logit coefficient larger than party identification twice (1982 and 1992), it has, on average, over one-half the power of party identification. When we compare the two economic items,

Table 5.2c

Senate Vote Choice: 1956–2002

Standardized Logistic Regression Coefficients

	1956	1958	1960	1964	1968	1972	1974	1976	1978	1980	1982
RETRO	.05	.07	.05	.06*	-.21*						
RGOV						.01	.05	-.02	.05	-.06	.01
PROSP	.16*	.11*	.22*	.08*	.16*	.11					
PGOV							.19*	.26*	.24*	.14	.38*
PPROB											
PECON											
RIRAN											
RWAR	.07			-.06*						-.17*	
RPOS		.08	.00								
PWAR	.17*		.27*	.20*						.09	
L/C						.02	.10	.19*	.08	.08	.13*
PARDON							.07	.05			
PID	.48*	.64*	.40*	.48*	.50*	.43*	.40*	.31*	.39*	.31*	.35*
SDEM	-.16*	-.28*	-.13	-.24*	-.04	.10	.00	-.15*	-.08	-.15*	-.29*
SREP	.04	-.04	.12	-.08*	.12*	.32*	.28*	.04	.16*	.06	.03

(continued)

Table 5.2c
(*continued*)

	1984	1986	1988	1990	1992	1994	1996	1998	2000	2002
RETRO										
RGOV	.08	.05	.08	.07	.09*	-.09*	.03			.08
RPROB								-.07	-.18*	
PROSP										
PGOV									.12	
PPROB	.20*	.30*	.20*							
PECON				.16*	.28*	.24*	.10	.05		.29*
RIRAN										
RWAR		.09								
RPOS	.10*		.01	-.01	.02	-.06	-.10	-.12*	-.03	.05
PWAR	.16*	.05	.09	.04	.08*				-.02	
FAFFAIRS							.13	.24*		
L/C	.01	.12	.19*	.18*	.22*	.27*	.29*	.14*	.30*	.26*
PID	.33*	.35*	.29*	.34*	.22*	.26*	.38*	.35*	.39*	.30*
SDEM	-.16*	-.00	-.13*	-.37*	-.13*	-.18*	-.07	-.11	-.23*	-.19*
SREP	.14*	.18	.24*	.01	.07	.06	.10	.18	.00	.04

Note: Asterisk (*) indicates significance at .05 level, 2-tailed or better.

we can see that the prospective items are more powerful than the retrospective items in all but three years (1968, 1998, and 2000). Moreover, if we look at the relative power of incumbency and the prospective items, we can see that with the exceptions of 1964 and 1998, the prospective economic item is more powerful than at least one of the two incumbency variables. Furthermore, the prospective item is more powerful than both incumbency items nine times out of the twenty-one opportunities.

The House and Senate

Are there similarities across the two chambers? Do they differ tremendously? The main pattern one observes is that the two chambers are very similar. When we look at the economic evaluations, we see that the same types of economic evaluations are important for the candidates of both chambers. Prospective economic evaluations are more important than their retrospective counterparts quite consistently, regardless of chamber. Incumbency, in general, is beneficial. The non-economic variables, such as party identification and ideology, are similar across the two levels. We also see that among the non-economic items that we can divide temporally there appears to be a similar pattern across the two chambers. In both the House and Senate, the prospective version tends to be more powerful. We should note that the retrospective item in 1980, the evaluation of President Carter's handling of the hostage crisis in Iran, is significant in explaining Senate vote choice, while the prospective war item is not significant. Putting the issue of statistical significance aside, the retrospective foreign affairs item is more powerful than the prospective war item. In the House election equation of 1980, we see the same pattern, but neither item is significant in the House equation. Nonetheless, the overall pattern is one of prospective items dominating retrospective ones.

There are, however, some differences worth noting. One that is relatively striking is the greater frequency of the prospective war items gaining statistical significance in the House equations than in the Senate equations. Despite the Senate's greater policymaking role in the realm of foreign affairs, these evaluations about the prospects of war appear to have a greater influence on voting behavior in House elections than in Senate elections. On the other side of the ledger, retrospections seem to be more important in Senate elections than in House elections. In 1964, 1980, 1984, and 1998 the retrospective foreign affairs items are significant in the Senate equations. These same retrospective foreign affairs items are significant but once (1998) in the House equations. It would seem that voters are holding members of the Senate responsible for what they might have done, but members of the House are being held accountable for what they might do in the realm of foreign affairs. We should not, however, make too much of this. Keep in mind that the retrospective foreign affairs items are significant in only four election years.

We can also note that the House equations appear to do a modestly better job of explaining the variation in vote choice than do the Senate equations. The average R-squared is .40 in the House equations and .37 in the Senate equations. While not a tremendous difference, it does point to the somewhat greater volatility of Senate elections. With their more visible contests that are more hotly contested, it is likely that idiosyncratic district-(state)-specific events will play a greater role in Senate elections than in House elections.

Conclusion

While there are some differences across the two chambers of the legislature, we should not lose sight of the similarities. In both types of contests, the prospective economic items dominate their retrospective counterparts. Also, the prospective items are quite powerful when compared to other influences on vote choice, such as party identification and incumbency. Regardless of the chamber we are examining, the prospective economic items are an important part of the explanation of the choices members of the electorate make. To illustrate this, one can simply look at the average change in the probabilities of voting for each party when the prospective items are moved from one extreme to the other. On average, movement from one extreme to the other on the prospective economic item for a year induces a change of .38 in the probability of voting for a particular party in the Senate contests. For House contests, movement from one extreme to the other on the prospective items for a year leads to a change of .35 in the probability of voting for a particular party.

What do the results mean? In short, the results strongly suggest that the voters are holding candidates for office accountable. Voting in legislative elections is purposive. The same evaluations that matter for presidential elections also play a role in legislative elections. Also, voters are not ignorant of the differences across levels of elections. Incumbency appears to be much more important in House elections than in Senate elections. Voters are paying some attention, however minimal, to the political world around them. They have opinions concerning the differences between the parties. More important, voters make connections between their opinions and their voting behavior.

Chapter 6

Economics and Politics
Egocentric or Sociotropic?

Earlier in this volume, I largely ignored the question of just what are these sociotropic evaluations. Now is the time to take this question head on. Since publication of the works of Kinder and Kiewiet (1979, 1981), students of political behavior have had to take into account the idea that voters might be sociotropic, rather than egocentric. We look at the available evidence on economic voting and find a disjuncture. At the aggregate level, election outcomes appeared to be strongly influenced by economic conditions (Bloom and Price 1975; Garand and Campbell 2000; Kramer 1971; Tufte 1975, 1978). While scholars found that different macroeconomic indicators influenced election outcomes, many, if not most, were also of the opinion that economics did influence voting behavior. When, however, the investigation turned to the micro-foundations of this phenomenon, the evidence was at best weak.[1] Economics might be related to election outcomes, but evidence that individual voters were basing their votes on the basis of economics was scant (Fiorina 1978; Sears and Lau 1983; Sniderman and Brody 1977).[2] The answer to this puzzle, according to Kinder and Kiewiet, is that voters are sociotropic. Kinder and Kiewiet found that voters in presidential and congressional elections appeared to be more focused on the economic condition of the nation, rather than themselves. Instead of looking at how their personal financial situation had changed and voting for the incumbent party if there had been an improvement and voting against the incumbent party if there was a decline, voters look at the national economy.[3] Voters reward the incumbent party for an improving national economy and punish the incumbent party for a faltering economy. In short, voters focus upon the collective, rather than the personal, when making political decisions.

While Kinder and Kiewiet (1979, 1981) have gone to great pains, especially in their more recent study, to make certain that the research community did not read their work as saying that voters are altruistic, a fair number of subsequent authors read as though they are making just that interpretation of the work on sociotropic politics. Here is a brief listing of what some authors have had to say on this point. Needless to say, this is not a review of the import of each of these works. Rather, it is simply a listing of what some have had to say about the meaning of sociotropic items. Rohrschneider (1990) in his examination of public opinion and new social movements argues that sociotropic evaluations and self-interested evaluations are distinct. Markus (1988) in his analysis of economics and elections *implies* that sociotropic evaluations indicate an orientation to societal needs, rather than personal needs. Alford and Legge (1984) in their examination of economics and vote choice in the Federal Republic of Germany argue that self-interest is not evident because voters are casting ballots with an eye toward sociotropic concerns. Stoker (1994) implies that sociotropic politics and self-interested politics are different. MacKuen (1983) argues that sociotropic concerns reflect a concern for society as a whole. Similarly, McAdams and Johannes (1983) argue that sociotropic evaluations are the equivalent of public regarding evaluations.

This is not to say that every scholar has assumed that sociotropic politics and self-interested politics are antonyms. Lane (1986, 316), for example, has argued that aside from altruism, there are several different interpretations of the sociotropic items. Unable to see the personal effects of public policy, people may use the national economic indicators as a means of assessing how the government has influenced their own well-being. If the national economy has improved, the role of the national government has probably been positive. If the national economy has deteriorated, the national government has probably done a poor job. Similarly, people may view the national economy as a collective good. For one to have low inflation, others must also benefit from it. Low inflation, or more generally, a healthy national economy, is an indivisible good. The extent to which one person is well-off influences the probability that others are well-off.

Welch and Hibbing (1992) implicitly make such an argument when they interpret the results of their analysis of whether men or women are more sociotropic. They argue that women may be more likely to be sociotropic voters than men because women see the world as being more interconnected than men. Lockerbie (1992) argues that voters may be using these sociotropic evaluations as a diagnostic tool for evaluating the performance of the incumbent party at providing personal prosperity. Miller and Wattenberg (1985) argue that these sociotropic items are related to vote choice, not because they reflect a concern with the well-being of others, but rather because they are politicized. Conover, Feldman, and

Knight (1987) make a similar, though not identical, argument when they state that these sociotropic items, especially the prospective ones, that mention the parties' names are hopelessly contaminated by partisanship.[4] Shah et al. (1999) make the quite simple argument, consistent with Kinder and Kiewiet (1979, 1981), that if a voter is using sociotropic evaluations, it simply means that the voter is making use of information that goes beyond one's own circumstances. Nagler and De Boef (1999) make the argument that voters are concerned with their own sector of the economy. Voters look at the immediate world and evaluate the president accordingly. If their sector of the economy has improved, they approve of the president. Conversely, if the wages of their sector have declined, they disapprove of the president. In short, voters are going beyond themselves to diagnose what the government has done to their own situation. Unlike Lane, Nagler and De Boef suggest that the locus is much closer to home.

The early tests of the egocentric/sociotropic nature of the electorate were hindered by data difficulties. The examinations of this question that have the strongest findings make use of sociotropic items that explicitly mention the government and egocentric items that make no mention of the government. In the terminology of Fiorina (1981), the egocentric items are simple economic evaluations, and the sociotropic items are mediated economic evaluations. It is not surprising that the tests show the sociotropic items consistently outperforming the egocentric items.[5] The following are some examples of the different questions employed in previous studies.[6]

Egocentric (Personal) Economic Items

"We are interested in how people are getting along financially these days. Would you say that you (and your family) are better off or worse off financially than you were a year ago?"

"Are you making as much money now as you were a year ago, or more, or less?"

"How satisfied are you with the income you (and your family) have?"

Sociotropic Economic Items

"As to the economic policy of the government—I mean steps taken to fight inflation or unemployment—would you say that the government is doing a good job, only a fair job, or a poor job?"

"Thinking about the steps that have been taken to fight inflation—would you say that the government has been doing a good job, only fair, or a poor job?"

"Would you say that at the present time business conditions are better or worse than they were a year ago?"

"Do you think the problems of inflation and unemployment would be better handled by the Democrats, by the Republicans, or about the same by both?"

Looking at these items, we can see that there are some important differences. First, as Kinder and Kiewiet (1981) point out, there is the distinction between the collective and the personal. Second, however, is the locus of responsibility. With the first set of questions, it is, at best, unclear who is responsible. The respondent is simply asked to evaluate his or her own financial situation. One could be quite pleased or displeased with the state of one's income without any attribution of responsibility to the government. One's income could have improved through the dint of one's own efforts. One's income could have suffered because one slacked off at work or a new competitor came along and undercut one's company's ability to turn a profit. A simplistic view of the egocentric model might be that voters are going to look at their respective wallets and reward or punish upon the basis of what is there. A more complex, and I argue more realistic, view is that voters look at what is in their wallet, untangle what is the government's responsibility and what is others' responsibility, and vote on the basis of what is in their wallet (or not there) that is attributed to the government.[7] Unless one attributes responsibility to the government for changes in one's financial well-being, we should not expect to see a relationship between these personal economic evaluations and vote choice or any other political evaluation.[8]

When we turn to the sociotropic items, we can see that they typically make reference to the government's role. Aside from the third question listed, either the government or the political parties are mentioned. It is not terribly surprising that these items are related to vote choice. The third item listed is without reference to the government. We should also note that it is among the weakest items in Kinder and Kiewiet's (1981) model of vote choice. The fourth item under the sociotropic heading mentions the political parties. Aside from getting at the egocentric/sociotropic distinction, this item also involves the retrospective/prospective distinction. Fiorina (1981) argues that this item is prospective, not retrospective. Similarly, in their discussion of retrospective and prospective voting, Miller and Wattenberg (1985) argue the results of their factor analysis demonstrate that this item loads most strongly on a prospective factor. Given the volume of work that shows the strength of the prospective evaluations on voting behavior (Kuklinski and West 1981; Abramowitz 1980; Lewis-Beck 1988a, 1988b; Lockerbie 1992; et al.), it is not startling to find that this item is strongly related to vote choice.

The 1992 American National Election Study is unique in that it contains egocentric and sociotropic items that are virtually identical, except for the following referents: the well-being of the national economy or the well-being of the person's financial situation. By making use of these two items, we can make certain that any differences that we observe are the result of the changing referent and not the other aspects of the questions. Here are the two survey items that are employed.[9]

> Retrospective Egocentric: "Over the past year have the economic policies of the federal government made you (and your family living here) better off, worse off, or haven't they made much of a difference either way? Is that much better (worse) off or somewhat better (worse) off?"
>
> Retrospective Sociotropic: "Over the past year would you say that the economic policies of the federal government have made the nation's economy better, worse, or haven't they made much of a difference either way? Would you say much better (worse) or somewhat better (worse)?"

There are only two differences between these two questions. The first difference, while inconsequential should be noted, is that one item includes the word "off" while the other does not. Second, and more important, is the changed referent. In the first question, the respondents are pointed toward their personal financial situation. Is the respondent better off or worse off? The second question points the respondent toward the national economy. Has it gotten better or worse? The major distinction between these two questions is where the respondents are directed. If these two items are placed in an equation explaining a political behavior or an attitude, we should be able to see if voters are directed inward or outward, or perhaps they are pulled in both directions.

Before we go too far, however, we should assess the degree of correspondence between these two items. If the collective items are simply a means of expressing what the respondent thinks the national government has done to one's personal financial situation, then we should see something approaching a one-to-one relationship between the two items. If this is the case and we put the two items in a model predicting some political outcome, we should encounter severe collinearity. To assess the degree of correspondence between these two items, the personal item is regressed on the sociotropic item. First, the ability of one to predict the other is low; the R-squared is .10 ($r = .31$). We can see that there is at most a modest relationship between these two items. Also, when we regress the egocentric item on the sociotropic item, the regression coefficient for the sociotropic item is 0.27. This indicates that there is not a one-to-one correspondence between the two items with error surrounding the predictions. The sociotropic item apparently is not simply a surrogate for one's evaluations of the national government's influence on one's personal financial situation.

What we should do now is use these two items to predict scores on several political variables. Using several items will give us greater confidence if the findings are consistent. If the findings are not consistent across several variables, any conclusions that are drawn will be tempered appropriately.[10] Regardless of the low relationship between the two items, we should examine the relationship of each to the dependent variables to follow controlling for the other. Perhaps what little shared variation that exists between the items also overlaps with the dependent variables. Consequently, by placing both items in the equations to follow, we can see if each exerts a unique influence on the dependent variables. Here, the dependent variables are presidential and House vote choice; adjusted Bush, Clinton, Democratic Party and Republican Party feeling thermometers, and Bush approval.[11]

As we can see in table 6.1, the simple two independent variable equations, both the egocentric and sociotropic retrospective items are statistically significant: the sociotropic every single time and the egocentric all but once.[12] Moreover, both of these items are of roughly equivalent power, as measured by the standardized coefficients. Just over one-half the time the sociotropic items are the more powerful. Nonetheless, when there are differences in the power of the items, the differences are rather minor. It appears, at first examination, people are concerned with both their own well-being and the well-being of the nation when they make political evaluations. At a minimum, it looks as though those who argue that we are much more sociotropic than egocentric were relying upon survey items that did not put the two ideas in a fair fight. The analysis clearly suggests that the egocentric items are of some consequence. At first examination, we appear to be both egocentric and sociotropic when acting in the political world.

The question now becomes why is the sociotropic item significantly related to these political variables when faced with the more narrowly constrained egocentric item. Clearly, once we've taken the egocentric item into account, there is not a clear explanation of the significance of this item in terms of self-interest. We should look back to the arguments about the meaning of the sociotropic items. Lane's (1986, 316) discussion of what the sociotropic items might mean is a good place to start this investigation. Here is a list of the various explanations that he offers.

1. Unable to see the personal implications of policies, people use the well-reported national news as evidence of their present or future well-being.

Table 6.1
Retrospective Egocentric and Sociotropic Items
Predicting Political Attitudes and Behaviors: 1992

	Pvote	Hvote	Bush	Clinton	Republican	Democrat	Bush Approval
Egocentric	.60/.24*	.36/.14*	5.64/.18*	-5.05/-.17*	4.46/.17*	-5.05/-.18*	.31/.21*
Sociotropic	.51/.23*	.45/.21*	5.26/.20*	-4.77/-.18*	3.21/.14*	-3.71/-.16*	.33/.25*
Incumbency		1.07/.49*					
Constant	-3.24*	-2.13*	-30.42*	26.61*	-22.82*	26.63*	.58*
R^2	.07	.15	.09	.08	.06	.08	.14
N	1303	1258	2253	2253	2253	2253	2294

Note: Pvote, (0 = Clinton vote, 1 = Bush vote), Hvote (0 = Democratic vote, 1 = Republican vote), Bush, Clinton, Republican, and Democrat (Feeling thermometer score—average of the four feeling thermometer scores), Bush Approval (1 = Strong Disapproval to 4 = Strong Approval), Egocentric and Sociotropic (1 = much worse to 5 = much better). Incumbency (-1 = Democratic incumbent, 0 = Open seat, 1 = Republican incumbent). The equations for Pvote and Hvote are logit equations. The equations for the other dependent variables are OLS regression equations. The standardized logit coefficients are calculated according to a formula found in Hilbe (1997). The first number presented is the unstandardized coefficient, the second number is the standardized coefficient, and * indicates significant at the .05 level, two-tailed. Note that the number of voters in the presidential election is less than that in the House elections. This is the result of only making use of those who voted for a major party contender. In other words, voters who cast a ballot for Perot (18 percent of those in the NES) in the presidential election are treated as missing data.

2. People's standards of well-being are inevitably comparative; the reports on national well-being are used for the purposes of social comparison.
3. People so identify with the good of others and national
   well-being that they take some satisfaction in "good news"
   and evidence that the nation is doing well; in that sense,
   what happens to the nation happens to the self.
4. Because people cannot achieve the benefits of such collective goods as peace and low inflation without others also
   benefiting, their self-interest is served by policies benefiting
   others as well as the self.
5. In a world of uncertainties and unknown probabilities, the
   degree to which others are well-off affects the probabilities
   that the self will be well-off.
6. As William James (1892–1961) wrote, the self embraces
   everything to which 'mine' applies: my brother-in-law; my
   wife's niece; a favorable national milieu serves my self-
   interest by serving those related others. Without using self-
   interest in the tautological sense, we can see that sociotropic
   politics serves a variety of self-interests including those of
   the altruistic version, caring about the fate of the nation.

Looking at these explanations, we can see that, to varying degrees,
there are some testable hypotheses. In number 1, for example, if people
are using the sociotropic items as some measure of their present well-
being, we should have seen no relationship between the sociotropic item
and the political items, once the egocentric item is in the mix. If, however,
people are using these sociotropic items as evidence of their future well-
being, it is not at all unreasonable to see both of them as related to the dependent variables in table 6.1. Lane suggests in numbers 3, 4, and 5 that
we might conceive of the sociotropic items as making reference to the national economy as a collective good. We as individuals benefit when the
national economy prospers. Last, in number 6, Lane suggests that sociotropic evaluations may be synonymous with altruism.

We can most easily test the second portion of Lane's suggestion in
number 1. If sociotropic evaluations are getting at people's expectations,
when we include expectations alongside them, the retrospective sociotropic
evaluation should wash out of any explanation of political attitudes and behavior. The egocentric evaluation, however, may or may not be reduced to
statistical insignificance. Below is the prospective item from the 1992 ANES.

Prospective: "Which party do you think would do a better
job of handling the nation's economy, the Democrats, the Republicans, or wouldn't there be much difference between them?"

Unfortunately, this item, while focused on the future, is also socio-tropic. At best, any conclusions drawn from an analysis of this item will be highly speculative. Nonetheless, the findings may lead us toward a greater understanding of what questions need to be asked in subsequent surveys so that we might get around this problem. If, however, the retro-spective sociotropic item still shows through as statistically significant, we will be able to discount both the first and second half of the first of Lane's six suggestions as to the meaning of these sociotropic items.

Looking at table 6.2, we can see that the findings are at best murky. In the presidential vote equation, the retrospective egocentric item is sig-nificant, but the retrospective sociotropic item is not. If we stopped here, we might conclude that the sociotropic item was tapping into people's ex-pectations, despite the retrospective wording. Fortunately, we have more to examine. In the House vote equation, only the sociotropic retrospec-tive item is significant. Looking at the feeling thermometers, we see that the egocentric item is significant at every opportunity and the sociotropic item is significant in three out of four opportunities.[13] Last, looking at ap-proval of President Bush, we see that both the retrospective items are sta-tistically significant. Comparing the relative power of these items also shows us that they are not terribly different. While the egocentric item is typically the more powerful of the two, the differences are relatively minor. In short, the conclusions we can draw at this point are by defini-tion tentative. The upside to all of this is we know more than if we had simply relied on a single dependent variable. Fortunately, by making use of several dependent variables, we are kept from quickly leaping to an er-roneous conclusion.

Before leaving this investigation, we should look at more fully de-veloped equations with these dependent variables. Specifically, we should add measures of ideology and party identification. The ideology measure is the standard liberal/conservative item asking respondents to place themselves along a 7-point scale ranging from extremely liberal to ex-tremely conservative. The party identification item is the traditional 3 point item (Democrat, Independent, Republican). By including these items we can get a better sense of how these economic items hold up when placed in a more thoroughly specified equation.

Table 6.3 looks much like one would expect. First, we look at the most straightforward finding. As one would expect, party identification and one's position along the liberal/conservative continuum are related to all these dependent variables in the conventional manner. Next, the prospective economic item is also related to all these dependent variables in the manner most would expect. When we turn to the two retrospective items, we still have a decided lack of clarity. In neither of the vote choice equations are these items statistically significant. Looking at the equa-tions for the Bush and Clinton thermometers, both the retrospective items

Table 6.2

Retrospective Egocentric, Sociotropic, and Prospective Items Predicting Political Attitudes and Behaviors: 1992

	Pvote	Hvote	Bush	Clinton	Republican	Democrat	Bush Approval
Egocentric	.28/.11*	.08/.03	2.67/.09*	−2.06/−.07*	1.91/.07*	−2.52/−.09*	.19/.13*
Sociotropic	.21/.10	.23/.10*	2.12/.08*	−1.85/−.07*	.68/.03	−.96/−.04*	.20/.15*
Incumbency		1.04/.48*					
Prospective	2.91/1.20*	1.31/.54*	18.99/.63*	−18.23/−.62*	15.90/.62*	−16.65/−.63*	.74/.51*
Constant	−7.18*	−3.35*	−49.38*	44.68*	−38.74*	43.45*	−.13
R^2	.47	.26	.46	.44	.41	.44	.38
N	1284	1231	2208	2208	2208	2208	2244

Note: All is as described in table 6.1, with the addition of Prospective (1 = Democrats better; 2 = no difference, 3 = Republicans better).

Table 6.3
Retrospective Egocentric, Sociotropic, Prospective Economic Evaluations, Ideology, and Party Identification Predicting Political Attitudes and Behaviors: 1992

	Pvote	Hvote	Bush	Clinton	Republican	Democrat	Bush Approval
Egocentric	.27/.11	−.02/−.01	2.52/.08*	−1.82/−.06*	1.34/.05*	−2.04/−.07*	.18/.12*
Sociotropic	.19/.09	.23/.11*	1.71/.06*	−1.45/−.05*	.30/.01	−.57/−.02	.18/.14*
Incumbency		1.00/.46*					
Prospective	2.26/.93*	.75/.31*	12.70/.42*	−12.43/−.42*	9.46/.37*	−9.73/−.37*	.49/.35*
Lib/Con	.80/.62*	.29/.22*	2.87/.18*	−2.80/−.18*	2.12/.15*	−2.20/−.15*	.11/.15*
Party Id	1.25/.54*	.84/.36*	7.19/.25*	−6.64/−.23*	8.07/.33*	−8.61/−.34*	.26/.19*
Constant	−10.48*	−4.12*	−55.08	50.30*	−40.66*	45.43*	−.34*
R²	.63	.34	.56	.53	.53	.56	.45
N	1022	1008	1678	1678	1678	1678	1681

Note: All is as described in table 6.2, with the addition of Lib/Con (1 = extremely liberal to 7 = extremely conservative) and Parry Id (0 = Democrat, 1 = Independent, and 2 = Republican).

are significant. When we turn to the thermometers for the two parties, only the egocentric economic evaluations are statistically significant. When we look at these retrospective items and assess their power, we see that the egocentric items are typically more powerful. That the egocentric items are more powerful should not be overstated. First, the differences between the egocentric and sociotropic retrospective items are not that large. Second, and perhaps more important, neither of the retrospective items looks terribly powerful when one also looks at any of the other items in the equations.

Conclusion

Regardless of what is thrown at the sociotropic items, we can see that there is support for the findings of Kinder and Kiewiet (1979, 1981). Sociotropic evaluations matter. When people make political evaluations, there does appear to be some attention paid to the political collective. The results of this analysis also show that the unimportance of egocentric evaluations is much exaggerated. The weakness of these egocentric items in earlier works appears to have been the result of the choice of items to measure retrospective egocentric economic evaluations. Here, with items that make reference to the government, retrospective egocentric items are strongly related to political evaluations. The results of the analysis reported here suggest, quite strongly, that people are concerned with both their own well-being and the well-being of others. We should keep in mind that even "extremists in the self-interest school" admit that a modest, very modest, portion of what we do is not motivated by selfishness (Mansbridge 1990, 12).[14] The results also suggest that we need to grapple theoretically with the question of why both egocentric and sociotropic concerns influence political evaluations.

From a pure self-interested perspective, the statistical significance of the sociotropic items when faced with egocentric items has been puzzling. Why should we expect individuals to be concerned with the well-being of others? Several potential explanations have been considered and all of them have left us wanting. Perhaps we look at the collective economy as an environment in which we reside. We can look upon our relation to the economy as akin to our relationship to our neighborhood. We want our home to be as nice as possible, but we also want our home to be in a nice neighborhood. We do not want to look out our front window and have a view of a cesspool. Consequently, we want our neighbors to have nice homes too. Similarly, we want to have economic prosperity for ourselves, but we want the comfort of being in a prosperous area. If nothing else, it provides us a certain security. We have less to fear if the overall economy is thriving. Moreover, if the economy is prosperous, we have a more pleasant environment in which to make use of our economic resources. While this is not necessarily pure altruism, it does express some concern for others. This well-being of your neighbors might entail some sacrifice on your own part, but not necessarily. It might be costless, or almost costless, for you.[15] Additionally, Becker (1976) argues that one might be better off in the long run if one acts altruistically today. While that may well be true, it is hard to reconcile that with genuine altruism. It instead seems like long run self-interest.

Regardless of what is motivating the electorate, we need to consider that there are multiple considerations that come into play. Moreover, these considerations may entail both self-interest and altruism. Most certainly, it appears that people are taking both egocentric and sociotropic evaluations (whatever each is exactly) into account when making political decisions.

Appendix 6.1
Retrospective Egocentric and Sociotropic Items
Predicting Political Attitudes: 1992

	Bush	Clinton	Republican	Democrat
Egocentric	6.93/.19*	−3.88/−.11*	5.84/.18*	−3.82/−.12*
Sociotropic	7.58/.24*	−2.24/−.08*	5.51/.20*	−1.24/−.05*
Constant	15.49*	72.04*	22.63*	72.14*
R^2	.12	.02	.09	.02
N	2338	2305	2288	2283

Note: Bush, Clinton, Republican, and Democrat (feeling thermometers scored 0−100). All else is as described in the tables.

Appendix 6.2
Retrospective Egocentric, Sociotropic, and Prospective Items
Predicting Political Attitudes: 1992

	Bush	Clinton	Republican	Democrat
Egocentric	4.07/.11*	−.78/−.02	3.42/.11*	−1.06/−.03
Sociotropic	4.65/.15*	.85/.03	3.11/.11*	−1.54/−.06*
Prospective	17.41/.49*	−19.71/.61*	14.31/.46*	−18.10/−.59*
Constant	−1.42	92.23*	9.03*	90.96*
R^2	.34	.36	.29	.35
N	2283	2254	2240	2236

Note: All is as described in this chapter.

Appendix 6.3
Retrospective Egocentric, Sociotropic, and Prospective Economic Evaluations, Ideology, and Party Identification Predicting Political Attitudes: 1992

	Bush	Clinton	Republican	Democrat
Egocentric	3.72/.10*	−.62/−.02	2.80/.09*	−.75/−.03
Sociotropic	4.09/.13*	1.05/.04	2.55/.09*	1.85/.05*
Prospective	11.11/.32*	−13.90/−.43*	7.86/.26*	−11.32/−.38*
Lib/Con	3.62/.19*	−2.12/−.12*	2.92/.18*	−1.47/−.09*
Party ID	6.62/.19*	−7.20/−.23*	7.46/.25*	−9.18/−.32*
Constant	−9.65*	95.47*	4.29*	90.59*
R^2	.43	.44	.38	.45
N	1705	1699	1693	1688

Note: All is as described above.

Chapter 7

Forecasting Elections

To this point, we have looked at voting behavior from the perspective of the individual voter. One aspect of this work, as with other works purporting to explain voting behavior, is that we are dealing with events after they have already occurred. We can take the American National Election Studies and make our statistical models fit the behavior of voters. While I would argue these endeavors are certainly worthwhile, as evidenced by my devoting most of a book to the topic, there are other ways in which we should examine the topic of voting behavior. We can study voting behavior by taking our models of voting behavior and using them to make forecasts of future events. Needless to say, I am not suggesting that we should try to forecast how individual voters will cast their ballots.[1] Instead, I am suggesting that we should take our micro-level models and translate them to the macro-level. We should try to forecast the actual outcomes of elections—who wins and by how much, who gains and by how much—across levels. Over the last couple of decades, there has been a cottage industry in political science concerning election forecasting. For example, at the 1994 meeting of the Southern Political Science Association, several participants offered their predictions of the midterm elections. Alas, not a single forecast was within twenty seats of being accurate.[2] Political scientists were much more successful at the 1996 meeting of the American Political Science Association. Every single member of the panel accurately forecast a Clinton victory in the presidential election. At the 2000 meeting of the American Political Science Association in late August, every political scientist on the panel correctly forecast a Democratic popular vote victory, with Jim Campbell at the low end with a forecast of 52.8 percent.[3]

Political pundits occasionally do better than the political scientists, but we should keep in mind that the pundits are able to revise their forecasts in light of new information right up until the election. In short, it seems as though they were paying attention to the latest polls and inside information. While these forecasts might be very accurate, they are hardly generalizable. They do not make their models available to us. Quite understandably, it seems pundits are reporting a gut feeling. Consequently, they do not provide us with the opportunity to test our models of voting behavior. All we learn, for the most part, is that a presidential candidate ahead in the polls the day before, or a few days before, the election typically wins on election day. I would hazard that one does not have to have any great insights into politics to make such a prediction. If we are going to wait a few days before the election to make our forecast, why not wait until the event itself? We do not think too much of someone's forecasting ability when he or she waits until the ninth inning of a baseball game to forecast the outcome. It just is not that difficult. Nor should we put too much stock in the forecasting ability of someone who forecasts the outcome of a presidential election hours, or even days, before the polls close.[4]

Aside from the simple thrill of making a forecast, there are other, more important, reasons to engage in forecasting. Assuming we move beyond the World Series rule and the Beaujolais rule, we can test our theories of political behavior without the benefit of hindsight.[5] While we might retool our models to fit the elections of the past, we are somewhat limited when forecasting. We cannot retool our models to fit something that has yet to occur. In fact, if we retool our models to fit an anomalous election from the past, we probably make it more likely that we are wrong with our forecast than if we had left well enough alone. Accordingly, we can put our theories of political behavior to the test with forecasting.

As the reader can tell, the focus of this book is the influence of economics, and economic evaluations, on elections. Accordingly, a forecasting model should have measures that take into account the retrospective and prospective aspects of economic voting, as described in the earlier chapters. There are two items we can make use of to assess the influence of the economy, more specifically, economic evaluations on the outcome of elections. Both of these survey items are from the Survey of Consumer Attitudes and Behavior. The *retrospective* item is "We're interested in how people are getting along financially these days. Would you say that you (and your family living there) are better off or worse off financially than you were a year ago." The *prospective* item is "Now looking ahead—do you think that a year from now you (and your family living there) will be better off financially, or worse off, or just about the same as now." In each instance, the score is the percentage saying worse. Unfortunately, in the aggregate case, the two items are correlated at .90, rendering them unfit for simultaneous inclusion in a regression equation. Using the percentage better did not ameliorate the problem of multicollinearity. Given this rather excessive multicollinearity, I can only make use of one of the two economic items. Since the prospective economic items showed themselves to be so powerful in the micro-level analyses earlier, I opt to make use of the prospective item here.

Aside from the economy, we should also take into account the potential for an incumbency advantage or a penalty for seeking to hold on to the office for too long. Some might argue that when a presidential candidate seeks reelection, he might have an advantage. Voters might be willing to give the individual the chance to fully implement his or her program. One term might not be enough. A third term for a party is another thing. After eight years, voters might be tired of a party. Also, it will not be the leader of the party seeking a third term, a la Franklin Roosevelt. Instead, it will be (or at least in recent history it has been) the incumbent vice president. At this point voters might be looking for a change, or at least sympathetic to the arguments of the opposition party. Similarly, even if the incumbent vice president has been victorious, voters might not be inclined to give one party sixteen years of uninterrupted power.

One decision that I have consciously made could possibly be buried in a note. Presidential popularity is not in the forecasting model. There are two reasons for its exclusion. First, the same processes that lead to presidential popularity also lead to the defeat or victory of the incumbent president. In fact, one reason we study presidential popularity is that we have a great deal of popularity data, but not much election data, to match up with our independent variables. Nannestad and Paldam (1994) in their review essay make the argument that these are largely the same by their intermingling of the vote functions and popularity functions in their discussion. Second, it would indeed seem strange to have a popular president defeated or an unpopular president reelected. Including presidential popularity on the right-hand side of the equation is akin to putting the dependent variable, somewhat attenuated, on the right-hand side of the equation.[6] If this decision is a mistake, the probability that elections are misforecast and the magnitude of the errors should be larger than they otherwise would be.

Presidential Election Results

How well does the model do when confronted with the data? Table 7.1 shows the regression equations forecasting each presidential election. Briefly, each line shows the year excluded from the equation, the regression coefficients for each of the variables in the equation, the forecasted vote without using the year at the beginning of the line to generate the forecast, then the actual two-party vote for the incumbent party, and last the absolute value of the forecast error. In short, the last column tells us how well the model forecast the outcome of that year's election without using that year's data to generate the regression equation.

Table 7.1
Presidential Forecasting Equations

Year	Next Year Worse	Term Two +	Constant	R^2	Forecasted Vote	Actual Vote	Absolute Error
1956	−.78	−7.99	64.49	.77	59.8	57.8	2.0
1960	−.75	−7.41	63.94	.77	51.3	49.9	1.4
1964	−.71	−7.20	63.11	.74	58.9	61.3	2.4
1968	−.75	−7.36	63.96	.77	51.3	49.6	1.7
1972	−.71	−6.78	62.74	.80	56.3	61.8	5.5
1976	−.74	−7.65	63.87	.76	48.8	48.9	0.1
1980	−.66	−7.70	63.23	.72	46.5	44.7	1.8
1984	−.73	−7.18	63.32	.77	56.2	59.2	3.0
1988	−.73	−8.22	63.69	.81	50.1	53.9	3.8
1992	−.77	−7.89	64.11	.75	45.2	46.5	1.3
1996	−.75	−7.92	64.20	.78	56.7	54.7	2.0
2000	−.76	−7.33	64.04	.78	52.1	50.2	1.9
2004	−.77	−8.59	65.02	.87	57.6	51.2	6.4
No year	−.74	−7.63	63.86	.78	56.7	51.2	5.5

Note: With the exception of 1980 Next Year Worse, everything is significant at the .01 level, one-tailed. Next Year Worse is significant at the .06 level, one-tailed, for 1980.

First, let's look at the individual coefficients. In every year, the length of time variable is in the expected direction and significant at the .01 level, two-tailed. Controlling for the economic item, seeking a third term or beyond is a rather difficult enterprise. The incumbent party loses at least 6.75 percentage points when it is in the position of seeking to go beyond two terms. In every year but one, the prospective economic item is significant at the .01 level, two-tailed the exception being 1980, where it is significant at the .11 level, two-tailed. Taking the economic item at its least powerful, we can see that the incumbent party loses right at .66 of a percentage point for every 1 percent of the electorate that is negative about the economic future. Usually, it is more like a .75 point loss.

Aside from looking at the individual variables, we can see that the forecasts are quite accurate. The R-squared shows that the simple two-variable equation explains approximately 75 percent of the variation in a two-party presidential vote. Even in 1980, with the less than strongly significant prospective item, the equation has an R-squared of .72. Does this model make any mistakes? Are any elections misforecast? Yes, the elections of 1960 and 1968 are misforecast. The model predicts that the incumbent will receive 51.3 percent of the vote in 1960, when, in fact, the incumbent party received 49.9 percent of the vote (absolute error of 1.4 percentage points). The model also forecasts that the incumbent will receive 51.3 percent of the vote in 1968, when it in fact received 49.6 percent (absolute error of 1.7 percentage points). Although the model does not accurately predict the outcome, the difference of under two percentage points is hardly a tremendous forecasting error. If we look at all of the forecasting errors, we can see that the average absolute forecasting error is 2.6 percentage points. One should also note that the last year is the worst year. In 2004, the model is off by over six percentage points. Even if we include the year 2004 in the analysis (the last row in the table) and look at the error for in-sample forecasting, the model is off by over five percentage points.

House and Senate Elections

In addition to presidential elections, political scientists also try to forecast legislative elections. We can take the same model applied to presidential elections and apply it to different dependent variables, specifically seat change in the House and Senate. While we might expect the same variables that influence presidential election outcomes to influence House and Senate election outcomes, we should note there are additional variables that one should take into account.

Besides the economic variables and the time a party has controlled the White House, we should also take into account the built-in advantage incumbents have in seeking reelection (Alford and Hibbing 1981; Collie 1981; Erikson 1972; Ferejohn 1977; Uslaner and Conway 1986; et al.).[7] Even in 1994, more than 90 percent of the incumbents who sought reelection won their contests. If we wish to make a forecast of congressional elections, we can safely assume that most incumbents will win. Open seat contests, however, are much more competitive. To take this into account, we should look at the number of open seat contests in each election, which can be gleaned from an inspection of *Congressional Quarterly Weekly Reports*. Knowing simply the number of open seats is not enough. We want to know what the swing should be in any year. In 1994, the greater the number of open seats, the more advantaged the Republican Party. Going back four years, the greater the number of open seats, the more advantaged the Democratic Party.

How can we assess whether an election year is good or bad for the incumbent party, while only using information that is available well before the election? First, as alluded to at the end of the preceding paragraph, we can safely assume that midterm elections are bad for the incumbent party; the regularity of midterm losses by the president's party is too obvious to ignore—1998 and 2002 are, of course, notable exceptions. What about on-year contests? Are these good years for the party that wins the presidency? That, of course, means that before we can make a forecast, the election will have taken place. Instead, we want information that is available well before the election. Lewis-Beck and Skalaban (1989) show that citizens are good forecasters of presidential election outcomes. When they examine the forecasting ability of the citizenry more closely, they find that when the election is a landslide, the percentage of those surveyed who forecast a victory for the winning party is quite high. To take into account whether an on-year is good for a particular party, we can simply observe whether a disproportionately large percentage (60% or more) of people pick a particular party as the likely victor in the presidential race. If more than 60 percent forecast a victory for the incumbent party, the number of open seats is multiplied by 1. If more than 60 percent forecast a victory for the challenging party, the number of open seats is multiplied by -1, as it is for the incumbent party in midterm election years. The more open seats there are in a good (bad) year for a party, the better (worse) that party should do in the legislative elections. From 1956 through 1992, it is relatively easy to construct this measure, as one can simply use the reports from the American National Election Studies that ask people to forecast the outcome of the presidential election. For the most recent election, one can make use of the reports in the popular press.[8] In 1996, for example, one can see this reported in the CBS News/*New York Times* poll conducted from March 31 through April 2, 1996.

Of course, we should expect the incumbent party to have an advantage in these open seat contests. We should note, however, the advantage is considerably less than if the incumbent were on the ballot. Consequently, the more open seats there are, the more likely a heavily advantaged presidential candidate's party, assuming one exists, will pick up seats in the legislature. Similarly, the more open seats there are in midterm races, the more likely the president's party will lose seats in the legislature.

How well does the modified presidential forecasting model do with legislative elections? It depends. Table 7.2 shows the equations for the House races. Here, the model does quite well. As with the presidential model, expectations concerning one's financial well-being are significant for all but four of the equations. In these four equations, the expectations are significant at the .21 level, two-tailed. The variable for the number of open seats interacting with whether the year is good is quite important. In a midterm election (by definition, a bad year for the incumbent presidential party) for example, every instance of three open seats leads, on average, to a pick-up of one seat for the opposition. This finding shows both how important incumbency is and that the incumbent party is advantaged in these open seats. The incumbent party still wins an overwhelming majority of these open seats, but these open seats also appear to be where the opposition can make some gains. Finally, time is spectacularly insignificant. How good a job does this model do in forecasting seat changes in the House? First, the R-squared is, on average, .52. Second, the average absolute in sample forecasting error is just over fifteen seats.

When we turn to the seat changes in the Senate, the model does less well. In fact, it bombs. The R-squared is below .20; the adjusted R-squared is below .10. The only item that offers a faint glimmer of success is that the prospective economic item is significant at the .16 level, two-tailed, and the open seat item is significant at the .20 level, two-tailed. Given that the equation does not perform well in a predictive sense, I shall spare the reader the table with the out-of-sample forecasts.

Conclusion

These forecasts speak to our models of voting behavior. As argued in earlier chapters, individual voters are looking to the future when casting their ballots. Rather than asking "What have you done for me lately?" voters instead appear to be asking "What will you do for me?" The patterns we observe in this chapter reflect what we saw in the earlier chapters. Presidential election outcomes are explained reasonably well. House elections are also relatively predictable events. Senate elections, in contrast, are

Table 7.2
House Forecasting Equations

Year	Next Year Worse	Time	Open	Constant	R^2	Forecast	Actual	Absolute Error
1954	−1.33*	.79	.32**	5.60	.51	−16	−19	3
1956	−1.38*	.73	.34**	7.03	.53	12	−2	14
1958	−1.43**	1.01	.29**	6.39	.54	−14	−49	35
1960	−1.21*	.55	.32**	4.65	.51	1	22	21
1962	−1.04	1.23	.36**	−.36	.55	−23	−1	22
1964	−1.22*	1.06	.29**	1.54	.47	12	37	25
1966	−1.64**	.99	.28**	8.76	.57	−8	−47	39
1968	−1.28*	.79	.33**	4.90	.52	−9	−5	4
1970	−1.32*	1.06	.34**	3.53	.53	−26	−12	14
1972	−1.30*	.80	.34**	5.44	.50	17	12	5
1974	−1.01	1.00	.32**	1.71	.47	−31	−49	18
1976	−1.31*	.81	.32**	5.12	.52	−2	1	3
1978	−1.49**	1.18	.35**	4.49	.55	−40	−15	25
1980	−.90	.82	.35**	1.62	.50	−18	−34	16

(continued)

Table 7.2
(continued)

Year	Next Year Worse	Time	Open	Constant	R^2	Forecast	Actual	Absolute Error
1982	−1.44*	1.03	.34**	5.07	.52	−40	−26	14
1984	−1.32*	.92	.31**	4.21	.51	4	14	10
1986	−1.32*	.75	.34**	5.10	.54	−22	−5	17
1988	−1.34*	1.04	.34**	5.02	.53	13	−2	15
1990	−1.31*	.82	.32**	5.13	.52	−10	−9	1
1992	−1.50**	.09	.31**	10.00	.53	−10	10	20
1994	−1.41**	.35	.29**	9.42	.51	−20	−52	32
1996	−1.28*	.77	.34**	5.64	.52	13	3	10
1998	−1.18	.80	.34**	3.52	.52	−9	4	13
2000	−1.32*	.87	.32**	5.10	.51	4	2	2
2002	−1.34*	.68	.34**	6.63	.52	14	5	9
2004	−1.30*	.90	.32**	4.24	.52	−5	4	9

Note: Asterisk (*) significant at .10, two-tailed; ** significant at .05, two-tailed. Variables are as described in this chapter.

much less explicable. We also see that incumbency is more important in House elections than in Senate elections. As it is frequently the case that the aggregate-level and individual-level findings do not match up, we should note that they do match up reasonably well here. Both the findings regarding the economic items and the incumbency items hold up across levels of analysis.

Aside from comporting well with the individual model of voting behavior developed in this work, these equations also lend support to the argument that elections are predictable events. By taking a few bits of information that are available *well* before the general election campaign begins in earnest, we can forecast the outcome of elections quite well. We can measure the time a party has controlled the White House as the previous election is called in the media, fully four years before the election we are trying to forecast. The only item that comes from the election year is the measure of voters' expectations concerning their personal financial well-being, and this is available before the parties' conventions. In short, we can make quite accurate forecasts before the parties have nominated their standard bearers.

Appendix 7.1
Data and Sources of Data

YEAR	PRES VOTE	SEAT CHANGE House	SEAT CHANGE Senate	CYEAR	NYWORSE	TIME	TERM2+	OPEN House	OPEN Senate
2004	51.4	4	4	30.00	9.67	4	0	0	0
2002		5	1	31.00	7.00	2	0	45	6
2000	50.2	2	-4	20.00	6.00	8	1	0	0
1998		4	0	18.33	5.67	6	0	-31	-5
1996	54.7	3	-2	27.66	10.00	4	0	50	15
1994		-52	-8	28.67	11.33	2	0	-51	-9
1992	46.5	10	0	39.00	14.33	12	1	0	0
1990		-9	-1	27.67	10.67	10	0	-29	-3
1988	53.9	-2	0	24.33	7.33	8	1	27	6
1986		-5	-8	24.67	12.33	6	0	-44	-6
1984	59.2	14	-2	25.33	9.67	4	0	27	4
1982		-26	1	40.33	19.00	2	0	-59	-3
1980	44.7	-34	-12	43.66	25.33	4	0	0	0
1978		-15	-3	30.66	17.67	2	0	-58	-13
1976	48.9	-1	0	22.00	10.00	8	1	0	0
1974		-49	-4	40.00	22.00	6	0	-52	-9
1972	61.2	12	-2	25.00	9.00	4	0	61	8
1970		-12	2	28.00	13.00	2	0	-44	-5
1968	49.6	-5	-5	18.00	7.00	8	1	-34	-10
1966		-47	-4	18.00	7.00	6	0	-39	-6
1964	61.3	37	1	21.00	6.00	4	0	47	3
1962		-1	3	22.00	6.00	2	0	-53	-5
1960	49.9	22	2	25.00	7.00	8	1	0	0
1958		-49	-15	30.00	10.00	6	0	-44	-8
1956	57.8	-2	-1	23.00	6.00	4	0	30	3
1954		-19	-2	31.00	9.00	2	0	-34	-8

Note: PRES VOTE (2-party vote) is from various issues of *America Votes*. SEAT CHANGE from 1954 through 1990 are provided in Lewis-Beck and Rice (1992). The 1992 and 1994 values for these items, save SEAT CHANGE is in Lewis-Beck and Wrighton (1994). SEAT CHANGE from 1996 forward is from *Congressional Quarterly Weekly Report*. CYEAR and NYWORSE are from the Survey of Consumer Attitudes and Behavior conducted by the Survey Research Center at the University of Michigan. TERM2+, TIME, and open-seat interaction items (OPEN) were calculated by the author.

Chapter 8

Concluding Remarks

What have we learned to this point? Are economic evaluations are an important influence on vote choice? Do they matter across a broad array of elections? Let me briefly review the findings. Yes! Economic evaluations are an important influence on vote choice across a broad array of elections. More specifically, prospective, rather than retrospective, economic evaluations appear to dominate vote choice. People are looking to the future when casting their ballots. What is especially intriguing is the similarity of the findings across types of elections and across time. Regardless of the type of election, be it Senate, House, or presidential, the prospective economic items show through as the more powerful of the two types of economic evaluations. Regardless of whether we look at the 1950s, the 1960s, the 1970s, the 1980s, or the 1990s, the prospective economic items are more powerful than the retrospective economic items. In some respects, the data are hammering us over the head. The consistency of the findings is remarkable.

What does the relative success of the prospective economic model mean for elections? Are they more or less meaningful than we thought them earlier? Do elections carry a mandate for action by the winners? To some extent yes, but, and this is an important but, elections do not carry a mandate for specific actions. All elections mean according to the prospective model, as put forward here, is that on balance the voters favored one set of promises over the other set of promises. We still cannot infer from an election outcome that all the winners policy proposals were favored by the electorate. In fact, we still cannot infer that any one of the policy proposals were favored by a majority of the electorate. Some people may well have voted for the winner for one issue position or promise while being vehemently opposed to a second promise. Yet another voter may have voted for the same candidate, the winner, because of the second promise, while vehemently opposed to the first promise. What we can say is that the voters were looking at competing candidates and selected the one candidate they as individuals found most appealing, or least distressing. Voters are looking at a package rather than an a la carte menu. To get the items one wants, one may well have to put up with some items one might not want at all. Instead of looking at just one side, the incumbent, voters are making a comparison between candidates.

The voters compare the candidates. Voters look at what they think both candidates will do in the future. Incumbents cannot rest on their laurels. Challengers cannot simply attack the failings of the incumbent. Challengers are not just there to hector the incumbents. Voters, looking to the future, select the candidate that provides the most beneficial mix of promises for the future. Consequently, both the incumbent and challenging parties have to make some credible promises about what they might do in the future.

What does the prospective model mean for the actions of politicians in office? The retrospective model argues that politicians have an incentive to perform well because voters will hold them accountable for the outcomes of their actions while in office. If the prospective model is an accurate description of how people vote, do politicians have less of an incentive to perform well in office? Should they care about the success or failure of the policies they propose? If only promises matter, why should incumbents worry about the consequences of what they do while in office? Politicians do have reason to worry about what they do while in office. First, as is noted earlier, the retrospective items are a direct influence on vote choice on occasion. If, however, that is all we had to encourage incumbents to behave with an eye to voters and their reactions, it would be a rather thin reed upon which to rely. After all, the retrospective items are only significant in a few years and when they are significant, they are nowhere near the strength of the prospective items.

While the retrospective items are not a strong direct influence on vote choice, they are a strong direct influence on the prospective items in most years. Consequently, they do have an influence on voting behavior, albeit an indirect influence. This is why incumbent politicians have to worry about their actual performance in office. The results of what they do in office are likely to influence what voters think they, or their party, will do in the future. Thus, the retrospective items have an indirect path to vote choice.

While retrospections are consequential, we should not lose sight of the finding that prospections are a more important influence on vote choice. Presumably, the promises made by candidates are having some influence on the expectations held by the electorate. One concern is that candidates are making promises without the intention of keeping them upon winning office. First, we should keep in mind that credibility is important. If a candidate makes a promise and then purposefully does not keep it, or if a candidate makes a series of promises and there is no discernable effort to keep any of them, voters will in all likelihood make note of that at the next election. This, of course, assumes that voters have the ability and the inclination to keep tabs on candidates. If we accept the argument that voters are paying attention to promises when casting ballots, it is not a large leap to assume that voters will pay attention to whether candidates follow through on their promises.

Aside from the logic that inclines us to believe voters will keep an eye on whether candidates follow through on their promises, we can also look to the behavior of candidates to see if they act as if voters are paying attention. Fishel (1985), for example, finds that presidential candidates do attempt to follow through on the vast majority of their promises upon taking office. Perhaps their promises are sincere desires to change public policy, so they have no personal difficulty in trying to move forward with the promises made in the campaign. Perhaps they do not care one way or the other about the promises they made during the campaign. The candidates may even be opposed to the promises made during the campaign. Nonetheless, they have an electoral incentive to attempt to keep their promises.

What would happen if candidates did not keep their promises? What if after an election, the winner simply discarded the campaign promises in a trash can? One would think, according to the logic of the model, voters would start discounting the promises made by candidates. If the winner reneged on promises made during the campaign, the opposition would have an easier time convincing the electorate that the incumbent was untrustworthy. If upon winning office, the voters find that the old opposition engaged in the same dissimulation, the voters would then have an incentive to become pure retrospective voters. If promises are not to be believed, voters will have to rely upon the concrete, the experiential. Voters under these circumstances will focus on the past performance of the incumbent administration rather than the promises of both parties' candidates.

Because voters appear to be looking to the future when casting their ballots, politicians have a different set of electoral incentives with which to contend than they would under a retrospective model. Instead of obsessively worrying about the short-term, incumbent politicians have an incentive to take a look at the long-term. Instead of trying, for example, to make the economy look good today, incumbents have an incentive to try to make the economy look good in the future. Therefore, we should not expect the incumbents to create political business cycles where they manipulate the economy so as to make it look good just as election day approaches only to fall into the abyss immediately following the election. If we as voters are concerned with the future, challenging politicians will have a similar incentive. Consequently, they will not promise actions that will have short-term benefits that will also have great long-term costs that we as voters can discern.

To conclude, voters are not simply looking to the past. The citizenry may not be terribly sophisticated (Converse 1964; Conover and Feldman 1989; Smith 1989; et al.) about issues, but neither are they uninformed about politics. They do make judgments about candidates for office that are related to issues of governance. They make judgments about what they think the candidates for office will do if they are able to win office. The choices voters make are directly related to issues of governance. In short, voters' choices are meaningful.

Notes

Chapter 1. Introduction

1. We should, of course, be careful about placing ourselves in the role of judges. After all, regardless of whether people are doing what we think they should be doing, democracy has been performing pretty well here for a long time.

2. More recently, we can note the exchange between Evans and Anderson (2006) and Lewis-Beck (2006) where they debated the amount of retrospective economic voting that takes place in the electorate.

3. See Miller and Wattenberg (1985) for a thorough discussion between the distinction of policy, or issue, voting and performance voting.

4. One might argue that the retrospective approach is satisficing rather than maximizing.

5. Of course, both models ignore the question of why people bother to turn out in the first place. See Downs (1957), Ferejohn and Fiorina (1974), Ledyard (1984), Palfrey and Rosenthal (1985), and Riker and Ordershook (1968). See also Grafstein (1991) for a evidential decision theory of turnout.

6. An individual might also prefer the government to do nothing. Inactivity might be preferable to the feasible alternatives.

7. See Popkin (1994) on the by-product theory of information. In brief, we get political information through our endeavors outside of politics and then take that information into account in the political world.

8. Moreover, by focusing on economics/finances, we can keep the model from being non-falsifiable.

9. The retrospective model argues that people try to maximize their well-being by rewarding or punishing the incumbent party. Because only the incumbent party is examined, it is nonetheless a satisficing approach, rather than a maximization approach. Looking at the range of plausible alternatives would be more akin to a maximization approach.

10. Fiorina (1981a) in his theoretical model of retrospective voting does state that voters attempt to calculate a value for the hypothetical performance of the opposition party if it were in office, but his empirical test of the model takes into account only evaluations of the incumbent party. Hibbs (1987) also develops a theoretical model in which voters take into account the likely performance of the opposition party. Moreover, his empirical model makes a first cut at incorporating those evaluations by making use of different constants for each presidency in his aggregate model.

11. Achen (1992, 199), for example, argues that retrospective voting is not consistent with rational choice theory. "The rational voter is a prospective voter, and the past is useful only for its clues about the future."

12. Even Norpoth (1996a, 802) in his rather scathing critique of the role of prospective evaluations on presidential approval states that "voters would be foolish not to ponder future performance in making political decisions." See also Haller and Norpoth's (1994) aggregate study on how people arrive at their economic forecasts. Here, they argue that voters are too sophisticated for adaptive expectations, but not sophisticated enough for rational expectations.

13. See Lewis-Beck (1988a) for a discussion of voter myopia and hyperopia. Briefly, a myopic voter looks to the recent past only. A hyperopic voter looks to the future. In game theory, the term "myopic" means looking only to the next iteration in the game. Hyperopia is not discussed.

14. The prospective model allows for a multiparty system. It is, however, easier to explain the prospective model using a two-party system. It is also most certainly easier to test using a two-party system.

15. This, of course, ignores the role of the opposition party.

16. Taking Key (1966) literally and perhaps further than he would approve would argue that the voter should not take such a promise into account, for the future is too unpredictable to forecast with any degree of certainty.

17. I imagine that if one is of the opinion that the retrospective model is an accurate description of the thought processes of the individual members of the citizenry, one does not think voters make this comparison at all.

18. For those interested in a highly detailed review of the literature, I suggest Monroe's (1979) and Feldman's (1985) articles. A more recent article by Lewis-Beck and Stegmaier (2000) updates the literature review. The authors also highlight some of the controversies that need to be addressed, such as the time frame and the locus of economic evaluations. The question of the time frame is the focus of this manuscript. There is some attention to the locus as well.

19. His later work (1981a, 1981b) finds more support for economic voting. This later work excludes party identification as an independent variable. He argues that to include party identification is to misspecify the model as it is putting something (party identification) on the right-hand side of the equation that is a summary of the other items (the retrospective items).

20. At the national level, the idiosyncratic events may well have cancelled each other out.

21. Miller and Wattenberg (1985) argue that these items are powerful because they contain a political referent, not because they are "sociotropic."

22. I have published works on this topic (Lockerbie 1991a, 1991b, 1992, 2002). I review, and expand upon, these in detail in the chapters that follow.

23. These are what Fiorina (1981a) refers to as mediated evaluations.

24. Of course, one could easily argue that since the election has not been held when these questions are asked, they would have to be conditional; it depends on which party wins.

25. The remainder picked Buchanan, Nader, or someone else.

26. Under a rational expectations approach, all that is key is that the expectations be unbiased. Here, so that these expectations might be taken as useful for political forecasting, I also argue that the error surrounding the forecasts is small.

27. Not surprisingly, this work uses the MacKuen et al. (1989) argument to justify the use of these items. There are, however, some additional tests employed later to get at this question in a more direct manner.

Chapter 2. Simple Economic Relationships

1. This, of course, assumes the White House is the focal point of evaluations of the national government.

2. This, of course, assumes that the two survey questions are identical except for the time frame, which they are not. Still, the findings are

informative on the point of which model of expectation formation accurately describes the process by which citizens arrive at their forecasts.

3. Even here, Downs (1957) argues that voters might vote for their least preferred candidate in an attempt to punish their favored party for moving away from their ideal point. The rationale for this behavior is that these voters are looking far into the future and attempting to pull their party toward them.

4. As the convention is such, the bivariate analysis shows Pearson's correlation coefficients, despite one of the variables, vote choice, being a dichotomy. Later, with the direct effects equations, the results are from Logistic Regression, an appropriate statistical technique when using a dichotomous dependent variable.

5. Keeping with the logic of the retrospective model, I phrase the discussion of this model with the voter either voting for or against the incumbent party.

6. We should note that this a period of divided government. Perhaps some of those who were of the opinion that the federal government had hurt their financial well-being were also of the opinion that it was the Republicans in Congress who were to blame.

7. For those who are interested, OLS regression shows the same pattern of results: the coefficients all have the same sign, the same coefficients that are significant, and the R-squares are similar. Now that we in the social sciences are using Logistic Regression so frequently, and since there are a reasonable array of supplemental statistics, we can make use of the more appropriate statistical technique.

8. See Menard (1995) for a thorough discussion of this procedure, especially pages 43 and 44. Briefly, one substitutes hypothetical values for the variables in the equation. One then takes the natural exponent of the total of this hypothetical equation and divides it by itself plus 1 to get the probability of scoring a 1 on the dependent variable for someone who has scores on the independent variables as stipulated by the researcher.

9. To further highlight Clinton's abilities as a politician, he does remarkably well among those who are both neutral about the Federal government's past performance and neutral about the parties' abilities to provide a prosperous future. Among this segment of the sample, the equation predicts approximately a .68 probability of supporting Clinton.

10. See especially Conover, Feldman, and Knight (1987) on this point.

Chapter 3. Party Indentification

1. This research question is still unresolved. One can look at the special issue of *Political Behavior* from 2002 and see articles by Achen, Bartels, and Fiorina that point to the continuing controversy over the nature of party identification.

2. I say virtually only because I could not find one, but there may be one out there.

3. For a comparison of the stability of party identification and other political attitudes, see Converse (1964) and Converse and Markus (1979).

4. If one is willing to argue that the party identification measure is interval, the Pearson's r is the appropriate measure. The typical Pearson's r is .80.

5. This, of course, ignores the idea of end-points.

6. See Weisberg and Smith (1991) on the point of aggregate movement in party identification making sense. It follows a pattern that is predicted by political events, rather than being simply a random fluctuation.

7. Alt (1983) finds the same for Great Britain.

8. Moreover, if I employ several specific policy items, the sample size will deteriorate. As it is, the inclusion of the liberal/conservative continuum reduces the sample size considerably.

9. This would also be a problem with using a change score as well.

10. We should note the R-squareds for ordered logit can vary tremendously. The R-squareds made use of here, for reasons of caution, are at the low end.

11. For those who are willing to make the assumption that the measures of party identification are interval, the ordinary least squares equations show much the same thing.

12. The McKelvey-Zavonia R-squareds are typically twice the size of those in the text. Rather than pick this R-squared out, I make use of the one provided as the default by Stata. Keep in mind that the R-squared is not the primary concern. Rather, I have a greater interest in whether the variables in the model are significantly related to the dependent variable.

13. As noted in chapter 2, the retrospective economic items do not have an explicitly political referent until the 1970s. The retrospective economic items in this chapter have a political referent starting in 1974. In this chapter, the retrospective economic item is first significant in 1976.

14. Variance inflation factors (VIF) indicate no serious problem with multicollinearity. None of the VIFs are above 2.00. See Fox (1991) for a discussion of regression diagnostics.

15. When we look at appendix II, we can see that the standardized coefficient for past party identification in each of the equations is larger than that of the prospective economic item. Nonetheless, we can also see that the standardized coefficient for the prospective item is becoming larger relative to past party identification over time. Also, the prospective item appears to be of consequence.

16. See Long and Freese (2001, 122–124) for a brief discussion of this procedure.

17. For the path leading from past party identification to current party identification, the coefficient is for the instrumental variable. As there is no reason to assume autocorrelation between past party identification and the other items in the equation, the coefficient for past party identification in these subsidiary equations is for actual past party identification.

18. Using the McKelvey-Zavonia R-square, the highest obtained R-square is .40, but typically the R-squares are below .30.

19. Here, the highest McKelvey-Zavonia R-square is .09.

Chapter 4. Presidential Elections

1. See Fiorina (1981a) for an exception. His vote equations purposely exclude party identification.

2. See Conover and Feldman (1984) and Stimson (2004) for a discussion of the symbolic meaning of the responses to the ideology item.

3. See Uslaner and Conway (1986) on this point as it regards the 1974 midterm elections.

4. The null model predicts 67 percent accurately.

5. The null model predicts 51 percent accurately.

6. Given the infrequent statistical significance of the retrospective items, multicollinearity is a concern. If there is an intercorrelation among the independent variables, as one would expect here, we should be on the lookout for the possibility that multicollinearity is masking a relationship between the retrospective economic items and presidential vote choice. To test for the possibility of multicollinearity, the logistic regres-

sion equations in table 4.1 were rerun using OLS regression. From this analysis, we can examine the degree of multicollinearity by looking at the variance inflation factors (VIF). As we are not concerned, here in particular, with the functional relationship between the independent variables and the dependent variable, but rather with the relationship among the independent variables, this statistical technique is appropriate (Menard 1995). The highest VIF is 2.18. Fox (1991) argues that the VIF needs to be above 3.00 for any serious concern with multicollinearity. Consequently, one can easily argue that the retrospective items are weak because they are in fact weak, not that they are weak because of multicollinearity.

7. If logit coefficients have a difficult time being interpreted, these coefficients that make use of two analytic strategies are even less clear as coefficients.

8. As this strategy mixes two analytic techniques, logistic regression and ordinary least squares regression, I also ran the analysis using ordinary least squares regression across the board. First, presidential vote choice was regressed on everything but the prospective evaluations. I then regressed the residuals from this equation on the prospective economic evaluations. Not surprisingly, the pattern of significance reported in the main body of the text was repeated in this supplemental analysis. Here the highest level of statistical significance was .001, two-tailed.

9. Becker delivered the address in 1992, but it was published in 1993. The emphasis is added. This quote is from a reprint of his lecture presented in his book *Accounting for Tastes* (1996).

10. Of course, one can imagine that one's expectations will color one's evaluations of the past. If one thinks the economy is going to improve in the future, one might as a consequence think the incumbent did a good job in the past. Nonetheless, by setting up the model in the fashion depicted in the figure, the prospective items, by definition, can have no more power than they did in the direct effects equation.

11. For 2000, this does not matter, as the prospective war item is unrelated to presidential vote choice.

12. I thank an anonymous reviewer for pushing me in this direction.

13. The results of this analysis are available from the author upon request.

14. The results are available from the author upon request.

Chapter 5. Congressional Elections

1. See the earlier chapters, especially chapter 1, for one explanation for the weak findings at the congressional level.

2. See Berry et al. (1998) for the argument that when measuring state ideology, we should be aware that elected officials of the same party in different regions of the nation may hold differing ideologies.

3. An unpopular president will, no doubt, find co-partisans frequently distance themselves from him. Of course, the opposition party candidates will do their best to tie these candidates to the president.

4. Of course, I would like to look at other levels, but that is problematic. Gubernatorial elections suggest themselves as a likely venue in which to test the hypotheses developed in this book. Unfortunately, the number of respondents in the ANES that report voting in the gubernatorial elections can be quite small. In many years, the number is less than 75.

5. See Lockerbie (1998) on the importance of looking at the partisan influence on the incumbency advantage.

6. Of course, we only examine contested seats here, as identified by the American National Elections Studies.

7. Zupan (1989), as cited in Jacobson (1990), points out that Republicans have smaller personal staffs and put fewer of them back in the district than do Democrats.

8. See Fiorina (1981b) for a statement of the argument that casework matters. He, however, does not make the argument that there is a party differential with this activity.

9. The prospective economic items are significant at the .08, .17, and .09 levels, two-tailed in 1960, 1978, and 1998 respectively.

Chapter 6. Economics and Politics

1. Note that most of the work that examines this disjuncture ignores the idea that voters might be looking to the future. The aggregate- and the individual-level measures scholars employ are both retrospective.

2. Theoretically, both outcomes are possible. The mass of voters might be voting without regard to economics. If, however, the swing voters, the voters who move from party to party from election to election, are voting on the basis of economics, we might well observe the phenomenon described. The swing voters might be consumed by economic con-

siderations. If, however, they are a small portion of the electorate, their economic voting will not show up in studies of individual voting choices.

3. We should, of course, note that the personal finance questions we employ encompass more than the survey respondent. The American National Election Study, for example, explicitly has the respondent include one's family members. Technically speaking, this is getting beyond a pure egocentric item. See Nagler and De Boef (1999) for an example of attention to the various groups of which people might consider themselves a part.

4. See MacKuen, Erikson, and Stimson (1989) for an argument that the party names presence in the survey item simply gives the respondent information. It related to vote choice because voters have some sense of what the parties will do in the future, not because of a partisan rationlization.

5. Miller and Wattenberg (1985) argue that the sociotropic items show through as statistically significant, not because they are collective, but rather because they mention the parties' names.

6. Kinder and Kiewiet (1981) have a listing of survey items from the ANES in the appendix to their article. I have selected from this appendix in drawing up this list of survey items.

7. I am not saying that people have an exact understanding of what the government is responsible for. Rather, I am saying that only if a person attributes responsibility to the government for changing financial conditions should we expect there to be a relationship between economic evaluations and political evaluations or vote choice.

8. Funk and García-Monet (1997) make such an argument. In their work, they first discern whether the respondent attributes responsibility to the government for changes in their financial well-being. Second, they look at the relationships between the simple retrospective economic item and political evaluations for this subset of the sample. As this assumes that all the changes that took place for a respondent in this subset of respondents are governmentally induced, it, no doubt, understates the relationship between economics and political evaluations. One can, for example, think the government has had a negative effect on one's finances, but at the same time experience an increase in one's financial well-being. In short, one might believe the government has limited the improvement in one's well-being. Alternatively, one could experience a downturn in one's financial well-being because one lost a job. Nonetheless, one might think the government has ameliorated this condition.

Consequently, one's evaluation of the government's performance may be just the opposite of that person's experience.

9. It would, of course, be preferable to have more than one item for each side. The ANES, however, does not contain such clearly worded items that are divided along the sociotropic/egocentric dimension aside from the items employed here.

10. See King, Keohane, and Verba (1994) for an argument on using multiple dependent variables as a check on one's hypotheses.

11. The feeling thermometers were adjusted by subtracting the average of the four feeling thermometer scores for the individual from the one under consideration. See Knight (1984) for a discussion of this procedure.

12. Because of the overwhelming amount of work that finds incumbency to be so powerful in House elections (Alford and Hibbing 1981; Bullock and Scicchitano 1982; Collie 1981; Cover 1977; Erikson 1972; Fiorina 1989; Johannes and McAdams 1981; Mayhew 1974; et al.), the House equations also include an incumbency variable.

13. When we look at the actual thermometers (see the appendixes to this chapter for this analysis), we find for the Bush feeling thermometer equation both the egocentric and sociotropic retrospective items are statistically significant. But for the Clinton thermometer equation, neither retrospective item is statistically significant in the expected direction. For the feeling thermometer for the Democratic Party, neither retrospective item is significant in the expected direction. In fact, the retrospective sociotropic item is significant in the unexpected direction. Given this perversely signed coefficient, I checked for the presence of multicollinearity. The highest VIF in this equation is below 2.00, thereby indicating the "wrong" signed coefficient is not the result of multicollinearity.

14. Mansbridge is referencing Tullock's (1976) assertion that most of our behavior is driven by selfishness.

15. See Monroe (1994) for the argument that altruism occurs only when it entails some cost.

Chapter 7. Forecasting Elections

1. One might quite reasonably argue that this is exactly what we do when we make use of the pre-election survey for the independent variables used to explain voting behavior as revealed in the post-election survey.

2. I should note that Jim Campbell did come the closest of the bunch with a forecasted gain for the Republicans of just under thirty seats.

3. My forecast offered at the panel was just a hair above Campbell's. I came in at 52.94 percent of the two-party vote for Gore. Unfortunately, I later noted a arithmetical error. My actual forecast was identical to Holbrook's at the other end—60.3 percent.

4. See Lewis-Beck (2005) for an evaluation of the forecasting models for the presidential election of 2004.

5. The World Series rule holds that if the American League wins the series, the Republican candidate will win the White House and vice versa. The Beaujolais rule holds that if the wine harvest is poor, then the Republican Party will win.

6. See Stone, Rapoport, and Atkeson (1995) for a similar argument. See Norpoth (1996b) for one example of a forecasting model that does not include presidential popularity. As an aside, a version of the model with presidential popularity from June of the election year included showed similar results to the model in the text. Presidential popularity is insignificant when placed alongside the other variables in the model.

7. Since we are now looking at on-year and off-year races, the two-terms-and-beyond measure does not seem appropriate. Instead, the equation includes the time the presidential party has controlled the White House; the longer a party has controlled the White House, the more likely they will have made some enemies.

8. Using the American National Election Studies for this variable is, of course, a violation of the dictate that we use only information available well before the election. Fortunately, as late, various polling organizations have started to employ this question and make the results known well before the election. As noted in the text, for 1996, the information is available well before the election.

References

Abramowitz, Alan I. 1980. "A Comparison of Voting for U.S. Senate and House of Representatives in 1978." *American Political Science Review* 74: 633–640.

Abramowitz, Alan I. 1985. "Economic Conditions, Presidential Popularity, and Voting Behavior in Midterm Congressional Elections." *Journal of Politics* 47:31–43.

Achen, Christopher H. 1992. "Social Psychology, Demographic Variables, and Linear Regression: Breaking the Iron Triangle in Voting Research." *Political Behavior* 14:195–211.

Achen, Christopher H. 2002. "Parental Socialization and Rational Party Identification." *Political Behavior* 24:151–170.

Alford, John R. and John R. Hibbing. 1981. "Increased Incumbency Advantage in the House." *Journal of Politics* 43:1042–1061.

Alford, John R. and Jerome S. Legge, Jr. 1984. "Economic Conditions and Individual Vote in the Federal Republic of Germany." *Journal of Politics* 46:1168–1181.

Alt, James A. 1983. "The Dynamics of Partisanship in Britain." In *Electoral Change in Advanced Industrial Societies*, ed. Paul Beck, Russell Dalton, and Scott Flanagan. Princeton: Princeton University Press.

American National Election Studies, 1956–2002.

Barnhart, John D. 1925. "Rainfall and the Populist Party in Nebraska." *American Political Science Review* 19:527–540.

Bartels, Larry M. 2002. "Beyond the Running Tally: Partisan Bias in Political Perceptions." *Political Behavior* 24:117–150.

141

Becker, Gary. (1993) 1996. *Accounting for Tastes*. Cambridge: Harvard University Press.

Begg, David K. H. 1982. *The Rational Expectations Revolution in Macro-economics: Theories and Evidence*. Baltimore: The Johns Hopkins University Press.

Berry, William, Evan Ringquist, Richard Fording and Russell Hanson. 1998. "Measuring Citizen and Government Ideology in the American States, 1960–1993." *American Journal of Political Science* 42:327–348.

Bloom, Harold and H. Douglas Price. 1975. "Voter Response to Short-Run Economic Conditions: The Asymmetric Effect of Prosperity and Recession." *American Political Science Review* 69:1240–1254.

Bratton, Kathleen. 1994. "Retrospective Voting and Future Expectations: The Case of the 1988 Budget Deficit and the 1988 Election." *American Politics Quarterly* 22:277–296.

Brody, Richard A. 1977. "Stability and Change in Party Identification: Presidential to Off-Years." Presented at the annual meeting of the American Political Science Association.

Brody, Richard A. and Paul M. Sniderman. 1977. "From Life Space to Polling Place: The Relevance of Personal Concerns for Voting Behavior. *British Journal of Political Science* 7:337–360.

Brunk, Gregory G. 1978. "The 1964 Attitude Leap Reconsidered." *Political Methodology* 5:347–359.

Bullock, Charles S. III and David Brady. 1983. "Party, Constituency, and Roll-Call Voting in the U.S. Senate." *Legislative Studies Quarterly* 8:29–44.

Bullock, Charles S. III and Michael J. Scicchitano. 1982. "Partisan Defections and Senate Incumbent Elections." *American Politics Quarterly* 10:447–458.

Cagan, Philip. 1956. "The Monetary Dynamics of Hyperinflation." In *Studies in the Quantity Theory of Money*, ed. Milton Friedman. Chicago: The University of Chicago Press.

Campbell, Angus, Philip E. Converse, Warren E. Miller, and Donald E. Stokes. 1960. *The American Voter*. New York: Wiley.

Chappell, Henry W., Jr. and William R. Keech. 1985. "A New View of Political Accountability for Economic Performance." *American Political Science Review* 79:10–27.

Clausen, Aage. 1973. How Congressmen Decide: A Policy Focus. New York: St. Martin's Press.

Collie, Melissa P. 1981. "Incumbency, Electoral Safety, and Turnover in the House of Representatives, 1952–1976." *American Political Science Review* 75:119–131.

Congressional Quarterly Weekly Report. 1996. Washington, D.C.: Congressional Quarterly, inc.

Conover, Pamela Johnston and Stanley Feldman. 1984. "How People Organize the Political World: A Schematic Model." *American Journal of Political Science* 28:95–126.

Conover, Pamela Johnston and Stanley Feldman. 1989. "Candidate Perception in an Ambiguous World: Campaigns, Cues, and Inference Processes." *American Journal of Political Science* 33:912–940.

Conover, Pamela Johnston, Stanley Feldman, and Kathleen Knight. 1987. "The Personal and Political Underpinnings of Economic Forecasts." *American Journal of Political Science* 31:559–583.

Converse, Philip E. 1964. "The Nature of Belief Systems in Mass Publics." In *Ideology and Discontent*, ed. David E. Apter. New York: The Free Press.

Converse, Philip E. and Gregory B. Markus. 1979. "Plus Ca Change . . . The New CPS Election Study Panel." *American Political Science Review* 73:32–49.

Cover, Albert D. 1977. "One Good Term Deserves Another: The Advantage of Incumbency in Congressional Elections." *American Journal of Political Science* 21:523–541.

Downs, Anthony. 1957. *An Economic Theory of Democracy.* New York: Harper and Row.

Erikson, Robert S. 1972. "Malapportionment, Gerrymandering, and Party Fortunes in Congressional Elections." *American Political Science Review* 66:1234–1245.

Evans, Geoffrey and Robert Anderson. 2006. "The Political Conditioning of Economic Perceptions." *Journal of Politics* 68:194–207.

Feldman, Stanley. 1982. "Economic Self-Interest and Political Behavior." *American Journal of Political Science* 26:446–466.

Feldman, Stanley. 1985. "Economic Self-Interest and the Vote: Evidence and Meaning." In *Economic Conditions and Electoral Outcomes: The United States and Western Europe*, ed. Heinz Eulau and Michael S. Lewis-Beck. New York: Agathon Press.

Ferejohn, John A. 1977. "On the Decline of Competition in Congressional Elections." *American Political Science Review* 71:166–176.

Ferejohn, John A. and Morris P. Fiorina. 1974. "The Paradox of Not Voting: A Decision Theoretic Analysis." *American Political Science Review* 68:525–536.

Fiorina, Morris P. 1978. "Economic Retrospective Voting in American National Elections: A Microanalysis." *American Journal of Political Science* 22:426–443.

Fiorina, Morris P. 1981a. *Retrospective Voting in American National Elections*. New Haven: Yale University Press.

Fiorina, Morris P. 1981b. "Some Problems in Studying the Effects of Resource Allocation in Congressional Elections." *American Journal of Political Science* 25:543–567.

Fiorina, Morris P. 1996. *Divided Government*. Needham Heights, Mass: Allyn and Bacon.

Fiorina, Morris P. 1989. *Congress: Keystone of the Washington Establishment*. New Haven: Yale University Press.

Fiorina, Morris P. 2002. "Parties and Partisanship: A 40-Year Retrospective." *Political Behavior* 24:93–116.

Fishel, Jeff. 1985. *Presidents and Promises*. Washington, D.C.: Congressional Quarterly Press.

Fox, John. 1991. *Regression Diagnostics*. Newbury Park: Sage Publications.

Funk, Carolyn L. and Patricia A. García-Monet. 1997. "The Relationship Between Personal and National Concerns in Public Perceptions about the Economy." *Political Research Quarterly* 50:317–342.

Garand, James C. and James E. Campbell. 2000. *Before the Vote: Forecasting American National Elections*. Beverly Hills: Sage Press.

Grafstein, Robert. 1991. "An Evidential Decision Theory of Turnout." *American Journal of Political Science* 35:989–1010.

Greenstein, Fred I. 1965. *Children and Politics*. New Haven: Yale University Press.

Haller, H. Brandon and Helmut Norpoth. 1994. "Let the Good Times Roll: The Economic Expectations of U.S. Voters." *American Journal of Political Science* 38:625–650.

Hibbs, Douglas A., Jr. 1987. *The American Political Economy*. Cambridge: Harvard University Press.

Hilbe, John. 1997. "Logistic Regression: Standardized coefficients and partial correlations." *Stata Technical Bulletin*, 35:162–163.

Hinckley, Barbara. 1981. *Congressional Elections*. Washington, D.C.: Congressional Quarterly Press.

Hyman, Herbert H. 1959. *Political Socialization*. Glencoe: The Free Press.

Jackson, John E. 1975. "Issues, Party Choices, and Presidential Votes." *American Journal of Political Science* 19:161–185.

Jacobson, Gary C. 1983. *The Politics of Congressional Elections*. Boston: Little Brown.

Jacobson, Gary C. 1990. *The Electoral Origins of Divided Government: Competition in U.S. House Elections, 1946–1988*. Boulder, CO: Westview Press.

Jacobson, Gary C. 2001. *The Politics of Congressional Elections*, 5th Edition. New York: Prentice Hall.

Johannes, John R. and John C. McAdams. 1981. "The Congressional Incumbency Effect: Is it Casework, Policy Compatibility, or Something Else? An Examination of the 1978 Election." *American Journal of Political Science* 25:512–542.

Jones, Charles O. 1981. "New Directions in U.S. Congressional Research." *Legislative Studies Quarterly* 6:455–468.

Key, V. O. 1966. *The Responsible Electorate*. Cambridge: Harvard University Press.

Kinder, Donald R. and D. Roderick Kiewiet. 1979. "Economic Discontent and Political Behavior: The Role of Personal Grievances and Collective Economic Judgments in Congressional Voting." *American Journal of Political Science* 79:10–27.

Kinder, Donald R. and D. Roderick Kiewiet. 1981. "Sociotropic Politics: The American Case." *British Journal of Politics* 11:129–161.

Kinder, Donald R. and Walter R. Mebane. 1983. "Politics and Economics in Everyday Life." In *The Political Process and Economic Change*, ed. Kristin B. Monroe. New York: Agathon Press.

King, Gary, Robert Keohane, and Sidney Verba. 1994. *Designing Social Inquiry: Scientific Inference in Qualitative Research*. Princeton: Princeton University Press.

Knight, Kathleen. 1984. "The Dimensionality of Partisan and Ideological Affect: The Influence of Positivity." *American Politics Quarterly* 12:305–334.

Kramer, Gerald H. 1971. "Short-Term Fluctuations in U.S. Voting Behavior in U.S. Voting Behavior, 1896–1964." *American Political Science Review* 65:131–143.

Kramer, Gerald H. 1983. "The Ecological Fallacy Revisited: Aggregate-versus Individual-Level Findings on Economics and Elections and Sociotropic Voting." *American Political Science Review* 77:92–111.

Kuklinski, James H. and Darrell M. West. 1981. "Economic Expectations and Voting Behavior in United States Senate and House Elections." *American Political Science Review* 75:436–447.

Lane, Robert. 1962. *Political Ideology*. New York: The Free Press.

Lane, Robert E. 1986. "What Are People Trying to Do with Their Schemata? The Question of Purpose." In *Political Cognition*, ed. Richard R. Lau and David O. Sears. Hillsdale, N.J.: Lawrence Erlbaum Associates, Inc.

Ledyard, John O. 1984. "The Pure Theory of Large Two-Candidate Elections." *Public Choice* 44:7–41.

Lewis-Beck, Michael S. 1988a. "Economics and the American Voter: Past, Present, Future." *Political Behavior* 10:5–21.

Lewis-Beck, Michael S. 1988b. *Economics and Elections: The Major Western Democracies*. Ann Arbor: University of Michigan Press.

Lewis-Beck, Michael S. 2005. "Election Forecasting: Principles and Practice," *British Journal of Politics and International Relations* 7:145–164.

Lewis-Beck, Michael S. 2006. "Does Economics Still Matter? Econometrics and the Vote." *Journal of Politics* 68:208–212.

Lewis-Beck, Michael S. and Tom Rice. 1992. *Forecasting Elections*. Washington, D.C.: Congressional Quarterly Press.

Lewis-Beck, Michael S. and Andrew Skalaban. 1989. "Citizen Forecasting: Can Voters See into the Future." *British Journal of Political Science* 19:146–153.

Lewis-Beck, Michael S. and M. Stegmaier. 2000. "Economic Determinants of Electoral Outcomes." *Annual Review of Political Science* 3:183–219.

Lewis-Beck, Michael S. and Charles Tien. 1996. "The Future in Forecasting: Prospective Presidential Models." *American Politics Quarterly* 24:468–491.

Lewis-Beck, Michael S. and J. Mark Wrighton. 1994. "A Republican Congress? Forecasts for 1994." *Public Opinions* 1:14–16.

Linden, Fabian. 1990. "The Consumer as Forecaster." *The Public Perspective* January/February:10–11.

Lockerbie, Brad. 1989. "Change in Party Identification: The Role of Prospective Economic Evaluations." *American Politics Quarterly* 17:291–311.

Lockerbie, Brad. 1991a. "Prospective Economic Voting in U.S. House Elections, 1956–1988." *Legislative Studies Quarterly* 16:239–262.

Lockerbie, Brad. 1991b. "The Temporal Pattern of Economic Evaluations and Vote Choice in Senate Elections." *Public Choice* 69:279–294.

Lockerbie, Brad. 1992. "Prospective Voting in Presidential Elections." *American Politics Quarterly* 20:308–325.

Lockerbie, Brad. 1998. "The Partisan Component to the Incumbency Advantage: 1956–1996." Presented at the annual meeting of the Midwest Political Science Association.

Lockerbie, Brad. 2002. "Party Identification: Constancy and Change." *American Politics Research* 30:384–405.

Long, J. Scott. 1997. *Regression Models for Categorical and Limited Dependent Variables.* Thousand Oaks: Sage Publications, Inc.

Long, J. Scott and Jeremy Freese. 2001. *Regression for Categorical Dependent Variables Using Stata.* College Station, TX: Stata Press.

MacKuen, Michael B. 1983. "Political Drama, Economic Conditions, and the Dynamics of Presidential Popularity." *American Journal of Political Science* 27:165–192.

MacKuen, Michael B., Robert S. Erikson, and James A. Stimson. 1989. "Macropartisanship." *American Political Science Review* 83:1125–1142.

Mann, Thomas E. 1978. *Unsafe at any Margin: Interpreting Congressional Elections.* Washington, D.C.: American Enterprise Institute.

Mann, Thomas E. and Raymond E. Wolfinger. 1980. "Candidates and Parties in Congressional Elections." *American Political Science Review* 74:617–632.

Mansbridge, Jane J. 1990. "The Rise and Fall of Self-Interest in the Explanation of Political Life." In *Beyond Self-Interest*, ed. Jane J. Mansbridge. Chicago: The University of Chicago Press.

Markus, Gregory B. 1988. "The Impact of Personal and National Economic Conditions on the Presidential Vote: A Pooled Cross-Sectional Analysis." *American Journal of Political Science* 32:137–154.

Markus, Gregory B. and Philip E. Converse. 1979. "A Dynamic Simultaneous Equation Model of Vote Choice." *American Political Science Review* 73:1055–1070.

McAdams, John C. and John R. Johannes. 1983. "The 1980 House Elections: Reexamining Some Theories in a Republican Year." *Journal of Politics* 45:143–162.

Menard, Scott. 1995. *Applied Logistic Regression Analysis*. Thousand Oaks: Sage Publications.

Miller, Arthur H. 1974. "Political Issues and Trust in Government: 1964–1970." *American Political Science Review* 68:951–972.

Miller, Arthur H. and Stephen A. Borrelli. 1991. "Confidence in Government During the 1980s." *American Politics Quarterly* 19:147–173.

Miller, Arthur H. and Martin P. Wattenberg. 1985. "Throwing the Rascals Out: Policy and Performance Evaluations of Presidential Candidates, 1952–1980." *American Political Science Review* 79:359–372.

Minford, Patrick and David Peel. 1983. *Rational Expectations and the New Macroeconomics*. Oxford: Martin Robertson.

Monroe, Kristin R. 1979. "Econometric Analyses of Electoral Behavior: A Critical Review." *Political Behavior* 1:137–174.

Monroe, Kristen Renwick. 1994. "A Fat Lady in a Corset: Altruism and Social Theory." *American Journal of Political Science* 38:861–893.

Mueller, John E. 1973. *War, Presidents and Public Opinion*. New York: John Wiley & Sons.

Nadeau, Richard and Michael S. Lewis-Beck. 2001. "National Economic Voting in U.S. Presidential Elections." *Journal of Politics* 63:159–181.

Nagler, Jonathon and Suzanna DeBoef. 1999. "Economic Voting: Enlightened Self-Interest and Economic Reference Groups." Paper presented at the Annual Meeting of the Midwest Political Science Association, April 1999, Chicago.

Nannestad, Peter and Martin Paldam. 1994. "The VP-Function: A Survey of the Literature on the Vote and Popularity Function after 25 Years." *Public Choice* 79:213–245.

Nie, Norman H. and Kristi Anderson. 1974. "Mass Belief Systems Revisited: Political Change and Attitude Structure." *Journal of Politics* 36:540–587.

Nie, Norman H. and James A. Rabjohn. 1979. "Revisiting Mass Belief Systems Revisited: Or, Doing Research Is Like Watching a Tennis Match." *American Journal of Political Science* 23:139–175.

Nie, Norman H., Sidney Verba, and John R. Petrocik. 1976. *The Changing American Voter*. Cambridge: Harvard University Press.

Niemi, Richard G. and M. Kent Jennings. 1991. "Issues and Inheritance in the Formation of Party Identification." *American Journal of Political Science* 35:970–988.

Niemi, Richard G., Richard S. Katz, and David Newman. 1980. "Reconstructing Past Partisanship: The Failure of the Party Identification Recall Questions." *American Journal of Political Science* 24:633–651.

Norpoth, Helmut. 1996a. "Rejoinder." *Journal of Politics*, 58:802–806.

Norpoth, Helmut. 1996b. "Of Time and Candidates: A Forecast for 1996." *American Politics Quarterly* 24:443–467.

Norpoth, Helmut. 2001. "Divided Government and Economic Voting." *Journal of Politics* 63:414–435.

Page, Benjamin I. and Calvin Jones. 1979. "Reciprocal Effects of Policy Preferences, Party Loyalties, and the Vote." *American Political Science Review* 73:1071–1089.

Palfrey, Thomas R. and Howard Rosenthal. 1985. "Voting Participation and Strategic Uncertainty." *American Political Science Review* 79:62–78.

Peffley, Mark. 1985. "The Voter as Juror: Attributing Responsibility for Economic Conditions." *Political Behavior* 6:275–294.

Popkin, Samuel L. 1994. *The Reasoning Voter: Communication and Persuasion in Presidential Campaigns*. Chicago: The University of Chicago Press.

Repass, David E. 1971. "Issue Salience and Party Choice." *American Political Science Review* 65:389–400.

Riker, William H. and Peter C. Ordeshook. 1968. "A Theory of the Calculus of Voting." *American Political Science Review* 62:28–42.

Rohrschneider, Robert. 1990. "The Roots of Public Opinion Toward New Social Movements: An Empirical Test of Competing Explanations." *American Journal of Political Science* 34:1–30.

Royed, Terry and Stephen Borrelli. 1997. "Political Parties and Public Policy: Social Welfare Policy from Carter to Bush." *Polity* 29:539–564.

Scammon, Richard. Various years. *America Votes*. Washington, D.C.: Congressional Quarterly Press.

Sears, David O. and Richard R. Lau. 1983. "Inducing Apparently Self-Interested Political Preferences." *American Political Science Review* 74:223–253.

Shah, Dhavan V., Mark D. Watts, David Domke, David P. Fan, and Michael Fibison. 1999. "News Coverage, Economic Cues, and the Public's Presidential Preferences, 1984–1996." *Journal of Politics* 61:914–943.

Smith, Eric R. A. N. 1989. *The Unchanging American Voter*. Berkeley: University of California Press.

Sniderman, Paul M. and Richard A. Brody. 1977. "Coping: The Ethic of Self-Reliance." *American Journal of Political Science* 21:501–521.

Stimson, James A. 2004. *Tides of Consent: How Public Opinion Shapes American Politics*. Cambridge: Cambridge University Press.

Stokes, Donald E. and Warren E. Miller. 1966. "Party Government and the Saliency of Congress." In *Elections and the Political Order*, ed. Angus Campbell, Philip E. Converse, Warren E. Miller, and Donald E. Stokes. New York: Wiley.

Stone, Walter J., Ronald B. Rapoport, and Lonna Rae Atkeson. 1995. "A Simulation Model of Presidential Nomination Choice." *American Journal of Political Science* 39:135–161.

Sullivan, John L., James Pierson, and George E. Marcus. 1978. "Ideological Constraint in the Mass Public: A Methodological Critique and Some New Findings. *American Journal of Political Science* 22:233–249.

Survey of Consumer Attitudes and Behavior, 1956–2004.

Tufte, Edward R. 1975. "Determinants of the Outcomes of Midterm Congressional Elections." *American Political Science Review* 69:812–826.

Tufte, Edward R. 1978. *Political Control of the Economy*. Princeton: Princeton University Press.

Tullock, Gordon. 1976. *The Vote Motive*. London: Institute for Economic Affairs.

U.S. Department of Commerce. 1993. National Income and Product Accounts of the United States, Volume 1, 1929–1958. Washington, D.C.: U.S. Government Printing Office.

U.S. Department of Commerce. 1993. *National Income and Product Accounts of the United States, Volume 2, 1959–1988.* Washington, D.C.: U.S. Government Printing Office.

U.S. Department of Commerce. 1996. *Statistical Abstract of the United States, 1996*, 116th edition. Washington, D.C.: U.S. Government Printing Office.

Uslaner, Eric M. and M. Margaret Conway. 1986. "Interpreting the 1974 Congressional Election." *American Political Science Review* 80:593–595.

Weisberg, Herbert and Smith, Charles E., Jr. 1991. The influence of the economy on party identification in the Reagan years. *Journal of Politics* 53:1077–1092.

Welch, Susan and John Hibbing. 1992. "Financial Conditions, Gender, and Voting in American National Elections." *Journal of Politics* 54:197–221.

Zupan, Mark A. 1989. "An Economic Explanation for the Existence and Nature of Political Ticket Splitting." University of Southern California School of Business.

Index